ENΓ

MW01243289

As I read through Ann's manuscript, the words of Paul in Ephesians 5:11 kept echoing in my heart and mind. I could hardly believe the level of depravity that humans have embraced. I was moved to tears at the damage that has been inflicted on our children and youth.

Ephesians 5:11–16:

Have nothing to do with the fruitless deeds of darkness, but rather expose them.
It is shameful even to mention what the disobedient do in secret.
But everything exposed by the light becomes visible—and everything that is illuminated becomes a light.
This is why it is said:

"Wake up, sleeper,
    rise from the dead,
    and Christ will shine on you."

Be very careful, then, how you live—not as unwise but as wise, making the most of every opportunity, because the days are evil.

Thanks, Ann, for your vulnerability in sharing the pain that you and your family have endured. Thanks for reminding us of the fact that the days we live in are evil, and thanks for exposing the deeds of darkness. It is time Christ's followers to wake up from our slumber, to protect our children and youth!

HAROLD ALBRECHT
MP, Kitchener-Conestoga, 2006–2019

Damaged is an account, just as riveting as it is heartbreaking, of a family's journey through unbelievable abuse and trauma—yet finding healing at the end. It conveys several powerful messages to us as we try to navigate our way through an increasingly dysfunctional world. As our culture moves ever further away from its biblical foundations, such stories will sadly become more and more common. Christians are supposed to be people with the answers, and this book will help us find some. Dr.

Gillies shows enormous courage as well as great integrity in writing this autobiographical account.

DAVID CAMPBELL
Theologian, author, and church leadership developer

Not for the faint of heart, Dr. Ann's life story is devastatingly difficult, even horrific in places. The heartache, heartbreak, and sheer evil is palpable at times. But the resilience, restoration, and recovery are equally as brilliant. Dr. Ann discloses an underworld that can even be cloaked in a thin veil of light, which is the worst kind of darkness. Most of all she provides us with an example of hope for the restoration of extremely broken people and extremely broken families in Jesus Christ.

KEVIN CAVANAUGH
Executive Director, FreeToCare | Calgary, Alberta

Dr. Gillies, in writing *Damaged,* has courageously exposed herself and, with permission, her family as examples of the human damage we are experiencing within our culture. Such damage is perpetuated by the spiritual and moral decline of a society that is trying its best to infiltrate the minds and souls of not only individuals but also groups of people gathering for their own pleasures.

Dr. Gillies challenges the reader with disturbing truth while awakening the reader to the evil we as humans can too easily succumb to. But she does not stop there. Hope is also offered. She offers spiritual and humanly practical advice to help reverse this destructive course of society. Her book is worth the read to awaken the reader and the Christian church to the atrocities of perversion and the hope we can offer through faith in action.

REV. DONALD M. PRINCE
Friend and former pastor

After years of guiding others to inner healing through her professional counselling, along with her intense, arduous sharing (through her previous books and speaking engagements) of her expertise and deep knowledge of gender dysphoria and related issues, Dr. Gillies finds herself ready to share her own traumatic history. I applaud her courage, her yearning to help others, and her heart for helping in the education of other professionals and the public. I definitely recommend this book, especially for those of us who recognize the brokenness and damage in ourselves and in those we know and love. Thank you, Ann!

ESTHER PRINGLE
Daughter of lifetime linguists/missionaries

In a chaotic world where all our relationships—with adults, children, animals, and things—are being progressively sexualized, Dr. Ann Gillies calls us to return to sanity and health. She shows us, from the intimate and painful details of her own family life, the profoundly destructive consequences when incest, sexual abuse, and perversion are hidden, denied out of shame and fear, and even protected and promoted by vested interests. This is an urgent call to vigilance and action for all who care about the well-being of children, of future generations, and of our civilization itself. A must read.

GEORGE R. SLATER, PH.D.
Pastoral counsellor and author of *Along Comes God*

Psychologist, trauma specialist, and pastor Dr. Ann Gillies' Damaged by the Predators Among Us is overwhelming! This book is skillfully written for easy reading, which softens the blows of the staggering stories of abuse at the hands of the highly damaged people who prey upon others, particularly defenseless children. So much hurt experienced by one extended family, including unbelievably dismissive and/or hurtful authority figures, courts, and schools included. Eye-opening, shocking, tear- and anger-provoking, Damaged also provides accounts of hope and healing while managing to give some laughs and joy along the journey.

ANDRE VAN MOL, M.D.
Board-certified family physician
Co-chair, Committee on Adolescent Sexuality,
American College of Pediatricians
Co-chair, Sexual and Gender Identity Task Force, Christian
Medical & Dental Association

Having known Ann and her family since the summer of 1976, I found this book a very hard read. In it Ann reveals the trials she and her children have endured. Ann has opened up a door that sheds light on the grim reality of the sexual predators that are among us.

Our home is meant to be a place of safety, refuge, protection, and security, especially for our children. Home is where we learn our life skills, ethics, and morality, and where a foundation is set for a good future. For Ann and her loved ones this was not the case.

Ann has fought hard for her family and for many others. She has studied and researched, and she continues to speak out as one with authority and a firsthand knowledge on the subject that this book covers.

I thank God for His redeeming grace in Ann's life. I remember the words of Joseph: "You intended to harm me, but God intended it for good to accomplish what is now being done, the saving of many lives" (Genesis 50:20, NIV).

Ann has survived with a right spirit and a heart for the hurting. My prayer is that this book will be to "the saving of many lives" by exposing a great and present evil in our society. May God give us clarity, wisdom, and boldness to speak out against such perpetrators!

PASTOR LOUIE FOSTER

Although the tragic happenings presented herein are extremely unsettling, Damaged is nonetheless an enthralling biographical account that one simply cannot put down until the final sentence has been read.

Dr. Ann Gillies is a trailblazer in her field, one who has had to fight to maintain both her life and her sanity from the very moment she was conceived in her mother's violated womb.

Ann's abusive betrayal by the very people who should have loved and protected her resulted in such a tumultuous and precarious life that she often wondered if she even belonged here. Ann has been dealt far more bad hands than most people could possibly ever deal with.

In this book she bares her raw, anguished soul, revealing traumatic experiences and emotional turmoil that no person should ever have to endure. How can anyone manage to get past such a harrowing life and still be able to get a firm grip on normality to help other people and even smile while sharing such hideous truth?

Her love for others who are also damaged—for all innocent children harmed by sexual predators—drove her forward as she dredged up from her crushed soul details to ensure that such unvarnished truths would bring help and healing to other fragmented individuals.

God in His powerful way has lifted Ann up from the miry clay and molded her into one of the most beautiful human beings one could ever meet. This is her story, a message from her restored heart to yours.

MARILYN JONES
President/CEO, Sid Roth Ministries, | Canada
Founder of Operation Rise | Canada

I wish to offer a sincere thank-you, Ann, to you, your family, and the other contributors for allowing us to walk in your shoes through the pages of *Damaged*.

This was not an easy read, but it needs to be told because, in your words, "most people are blissfully going about life unaware." Hopefully all who read this book will be motivated to take action, even in small ways, to right the wrongs being perpetrated against our most vulnerable.

HEATHER WIGHT
Former high school teacher

In *Damaged by the Predators Among Us,* Ann speaks to the horrors of the sexualizing of our children. Therefore, this book is not for the faint of heart. It is a must-read, though, especially by parents, the guardians and shepherds of children, who are supposed to love, cherish, and protect them. It is raw and honest, allowing the reader to "walk in the shoes" of Ann's children and other victims damaged by the same predator, her former husband.

We often don't understand why people do what they do. *This book is evidence of how damaged children will act, trying to numb the pain of physical and emotional scars.* Ann's work and research point out how the normalization of perversion is rising in our society, thus grooming our children in schools and through social media to accept pedophilic interests. This book will help the reader recognize and become vigilant to such evil, which is already running so deeply in our society. It has come into our homes.

Although Ann recognizes that the scars of abuse will always be evident through victims' memories, the book offers hope. She shares how the Lord has healed and is continuing to heal her family, restoring the mosaic one piece at a time.

In her closing remarks, she calls us to action. There are many predators among us. We can no longer sit back and only be observers but must get involved. In this way, we will help protect our children, the precious gifts God gave us to love and protect. It is our duty and responsibility.

WILNA VAN BEEK
Friend and Author of *When Gay Comes Home: Learning to Build Bridges*
Founder and Leader of God Gazers – Bridge Builders Ministry
Godgazers.com

The formidable credentials and personal testimony of Dr. Ann Gillies and her (now adult) children cannot be ignored.

Unapologetically describing the evil they endured at the hands of a family member, a sexual predator and pedophile, this book is a much-needed sword to combat the destructive propaganda, propagated by many in the LGBT community and supported by left-wing media and minds, by which "minor-attracted persons" that seek "inter-generational intimacy"—namely, pedophiles—are welcomed. The testimonies shared in this book are harrowing; the brutality of the pedophile, openly evil and chilling; the betrayals by the very systems put in place to protect the child, unexplainable and incomprehensible; the devastation in both childhood and adulthood, all too evident; the consequences of turning a blind eye, tragic.

Dr. Ann Gillies does not shy away from the demonic and mental holds within the pedophile, the links with deviant pornography and other sexual practices. And with over eleven years experience in working with sex-offenders and pedophiles, Dr. Gillies brings to this book evidenced-based analyses that are hard-hitting, with fundamental truth after fundamental truth.

This book is a warning. Pedophilia is morally wrong and any push to normalize this practice is saturated spiritually by evil and scientifically ignores evidence-based trauma research that pedophilia inflicts in childhood and later on in adulthood. As an experienced trauma specialist, Dr. Gillies is brutally honest regarding the effects of pedophilia, the sexual predatory nature of the pedophile and the role of pornography in this. She understands the need for counselling and pastoral care, the need to rectify not just the physical but also the spiritual pain and devastation, anguish and torment left on the victim. As Jesus said in John 10:10, "The thief (devil) came to steal, kill and destroy, but I came to give life and life in its abundance."

DR. ELENE HARALAMBOUS, Ph.D., *Genetics*
MSc, *Immunology and Immunogenetics*
BSc, *Applied Biological Sciences*
Professional Developmental Administrator, International
Federation of Therapeutic and Counselling Choice
Volunteer Lead Prayer Minister

DAMAGED
BY THE
PREDATORS
AMONG US

Ann E. Gillies Ph.D.

Damaged by the Predators Among Us Copyright © 2022 by Ann E. Gillies Ph.D. All Rights Reserved.

Disclaimer: Names have been changed to protect privacy.

ISBN 9798366497299

Scriptures taken from the Holy Bible, New International Version®, NIV®. Copyright © 1973, 1978, 1984, 2011 by Biblica, Inc.™ Used by permission of Zondervan. All rights reserved worldwide. www.zondervan.com The "NIV" and "New International Version" are trademarks registered in the United States Patent and Trademark Office by Biblica, Inc.™

Interior Design + Cover Design by Sarah ONeal | evecustomartwork.com

Edited by Cherilyn Johnson | Sparrow's Nest Communications

Available on Amazon

———

This book is dedicated first and foremost to my beautiful children
each one of you had my heart from the first heartbeat.
I also wish to dedicate it to the other survivors who told their stories
and to those whose stories remain untold.
May God give you peace in the midst of the pain.

———

Writers, by their very nature, spend their time
thinking about, wondering about, delving into,
trying to understand the very things that the rest
of the world doesn't like to think about.

HARRY CREWS

PRELUDE

This book is a compilation of memories and facts regarding the greatest taboo, pedophilia: the grooming and horrendous abuse of children. It is a book about the very things that the rest of the world doesn't like to think about. Everyone has a story... This is ours.

This is not a book that I looked forward to writing. It is a book of self-disclosure and exposure. The story you are about to read spans six decades. I set the scene with my own early life experience and show how an adverse early life can make us vulnerable and easily manipulated. It is a behind-the-scenes look at the effects on children who have been targeted, groomed, and violated by sexual predators.

A sexual predator is a person who has committed a sexually violent offense and is likely to commit more offenses. When the sexual predator targets prepubescent children, that individual is called a pedophile.

The memories etched in my mind and the experiences of my children capture a myriad of emotions—among them, deep anger and a sense of hopelessness. It has taken me over forty-five years to begin writing about these memories. It's difficult to put on paper what has happened. It's one thing to talk to a trusted friend and give them bits and pieces here and there, but quite another to put the whole story together in order to expose the truth.

What you will find in these pages is raw honesty. It's not just my story, but a story that has taken place in the lives of many women and children in all economic spheres and across all nations for eons. It is a story that must be told, because the safety of children worldwide is being compromised, at a rate the world has never previously experienced. It's a story of unwarranted trust, merciless manipulation, and determined deception.

But this isn't just my story. More important is the story of my children—how they were groomed and preyed upon under my own roof. It is the story of others violated by the same predator, whom I called husband.

Along with this, I open the window to the reality of childhood grooming, sexual abuse, and the darkness of deviancy that surrounds us, while parents focus on their busy lives, largely unaware. The news has been saturated in the early 2000s with new revelations about child grooming and pedophilia.

Our most trusted institutions are rife with pornographic and pedophilic scandal. The infiltration of predators knows no limit. As I write this, horrendous details of sexual abuse of children at Disneyland are beginning to come to light. I expect there will be much more to this story revealed over the coming years.

In 2017, I wrote *Closing the Floodgates: Setting the Record Straight on Gender and Sexuality*. Recently, Fox News carried a story on the grooming happening in our public school system. They could have taken the pages from my book.

While I touched on the issue of pedophilia in 2017, this current writing serves to expose the dark and hidden agenda of grooming. Activists are pushing the envelope by tutoring young minds and the entire populace into accepting all and every kind of deviancy as normative and setting the stage for increased child abuse. Activists now display their sexuality in front of young, impressionable children in our schools. While we once expected teachers to be circumspect—there's a word recently annihilated from our vocabulary—now we can expect just the opposite.

But I digress. I write because I cannot stay silent. I write to expose the things hidden in the darkness. Some of these hideous travesties are happening in families, as they did in ours; others are perpetrated by leaders the children trust; and still others by the predators who would steal children, kidnapping them to be placed in a world of sex slavery.

It's happening in our neighbourhoods, on our watch, and most people are blissfully going about life unaware.

The unconscious need for safety, security, and significance will often predispose children to become easy targets for manipulation. What was true in the last sixty-plus years is even more predominant now. Young people are increasingly ill equipped to see through smooth-talking schemers and seem more easily led astray than ever before.

From a clinical perspective, my family's story is one of disrupted and disorganized attachment, abuse, addiction, mental illness, and childhood adversity. May our story motivate you to action.

part one

BELONGING

1

I Don't Belong

I could feel tears welling up as I listened to my dad speak. It didn't matter that he'd been drinking most of the day; his words stunned me. His words cut me to the quick.

"You're not mine, you know."

What? What are you talking about? I felt my stomach churning and my heart began to palpitate.

"You're my dad!"

"No, no, I'm not your father."

My stomach continued to churn. There were times when I was terrified of my dad, and perhaps even hated him. But I loved him. What did all of this mean? And how could a nine-year-old process such a revelation?

Apparently Mom had heard him and was pretty upset. "That was uncalled for!"

"Okay, but what does he mean?"

Mom looked at me and said, "It doesn't matter. We can talk about this when you are older."

I looked at both of them in dismay, knowing that there was no use in pursuing this. Dad refused to make eye contact with me and hung his head. Mom, on the other hand, had daggers in her eyes.

I was left with unanswered questions and conflicting emotions.

Talk about it when I'm older? My world is collapsing, and you want to talk to me about it when I'm older? My mind was swirling. *What does it mean for me? I don't belong here? Where do I belong? Is she my mom?*

I turned away from them both, opened the door, and headed outside to my quiet place—past the garden and the huge rock at the foot of the hill, and up through the trees to the hilltop, where I could sob. It certainly wasn't the first time I'd spent time alone in my refuge.

2

Changes

Have you ever had a discussion with a three-year-old? If you haven't, I believe you just might be missing out on some of the most delightful interactions you could ever have. Talking with a three-year-old will challenge your world. You'll learn about life, nature, favourite colours, Mom, Dad, Grandpa, God...and whatever else might be on their mind at any given time.

Simply put, three-year-olds are enchanting. Just watch *America's Funniest Home Videos* or search on YouTube and you're bound to see at least one clip of a three-year-old describing life in great poetic detail. Their minds are free to wander, uninhibited by adult sophistication. And wander they do. If you can let yourself wander with them, you'll find a mixed world of fantasy and reality that, once left behind, is never regained.

This is a world of wonder, amazement, trust, love, enthusiasm, eagerness, anticipation, opinion, and dreaming. It is truly a time of life that is unique and indescribable. Three-year-olds are ever hopeful. They are often so excited that getting them to sleep at night can be a challenge. Promising them an adventure tomorrow might do the trick, but don't count on it.

Three-year-olds have no control over their future. They are open books ready to embrace life. Things they've experienced and learned can often be conflicting: love, acceptance, excitement, rejection, fear, and pain can be confusing.

———————

For much of my life I had no memory of what follows; the first three years of my life were completely lost to me.

In retrospect, I can see that I was blessed in my earlier years. As a three-year-old, I didn't know that the people I lived with, these people I loved, weren't my biological parents. What does a three-year-old know about biology? They were my mom and dad.

I'd lived with them since I was two weeks old, having been placed there through child services. Dad was the local doctor and Mom kept the home running. Two teen boys almost completed the family, but they longed for a little girl. I became available for fostering.

According to what little I've been told, life was predictable and safe. My parents were loving and kind, and my two brothers adored me. According to what I was later told, I was the focus of the family. My parents had their little girl and were thrilled. By all accounts I was a typical three-year-old...well, maybe a little more spirited than most.

But my life was about to change, and quickly. Although my foster parents had been screened and approved by the adoption agency with all documents completed, a clause had been added, granting my birth mother permanent custody within three and a half years of surrendering me to my foster parents, provided she married.

In 1958, my early childhood was suddenly turned upside down.

On a dreary day in mid-March, my birth mother re-entered my life along with her new husband, my soon-to-be adoptive dad. I had apparently been introduced to them two weeks earlier when they had visited. Now they had returned to take me away.

Bewildered, I was ripped away from the only parents I knew.

I have no memory of leaving my foster family that momentous day. I only know the deep sense of loss I carried with me well into my thirties. Even as I write this, I feel sadness well up in my heart.

Fast forward thirty-four years. When I was thirty-seven, I was able to reconnect with Margaret, my foster mom. She was a lovely lady in her late eighties at that time. Her husband had died several years before. We spent a wonderful afternoon together as she reminisced. Talking about this conversation still stirs my emotions. This is a picture taken on that day.

Margaret told me I had been a lively, loving, and kind child. I was happy to learn that they'd had their own beautiful little girl just six months after I left. It was like God heard the cry of their hearts and gave them the child they had longed for.

Margaret told me that my birth mother and her husband and I had returned for a visit a year after I had been taken away. When she was preparing dinner that night for all of us, she exclaimed, "Oh, I need some potatoes." Immediately I ran toward the basement door to get the potatoes for her. I had not forgotten where things were kept in their home even a year later. Although I have no recollection of this visit when I was four and a half, describing it now stirs deep emotional pain.

Margaret also filled in the details of what had happened the day I left their home, so many years before.

> When your mom and dad came to get you that day, you refused to go with them in their car. I had to send Glen with you in their car and they drove around for hours until you finally fell asleep. Garnet and Freda (my new mom and dad) brought Glen back and then drove away, with you sleeping in the back seat.

Although my foster mom didn't say so, I expect I may have become quite emotional and resistant. I did not know these people, and I don't know any three-year-old who would be willing or wanting to get into a car with two people she didn't know. I must have put up quite a stink to have my foster brother Glen end up sitting in the car beside me.

When I heard the details of this event the thought crossed my mind, *I don't want to go.* It was almost like I was hearing that three-year-old speak.

3

Loss

My foster parents lost their daughter that day in March, and their sons, Dwight and Glen, lost their baby sister. I lost the only family I had ever known.

I now had two moms who loved me, and both wanted to keep me. How difficult that must have been for both of them. I'm positive each family was praying that the judge would rule in their favor. Sadly, only one can win in such situations, but what does a three-year-old know about any of these things?

I had no understanding of what had happened, but the reality was that I was taken from the only home I had ever known and the parents who loved me, to a new home—my forever home.

It was a difficult time for everyone involved and definitely the most traumatic of my young life. Everyone was in tears. No matter how many kind words they may have spoken, I refused to be consoled.

After I fell asleep in that car with my foster brother beside me, I can't imagine how horrific it must have been when I awoke in a strange place with two strangers. How terrified I must have been.

My new mom later told me that I cried solidly for the next two

weeks. Yep, taking a child away from their home, parents, brothers, and safety will do that. I cried myself to sleep each night, longing for the familiar, for my family. I was grieving.

My birth mom and her husband, although thrilled to have me, were conflicted. On the one hand they had me, their hearts' desire; on the other hand, they were saddened to take me from the folks who had taken such good care of me and loved me as their own.

Getting me home was one thing; living with me the next few weeks must have been stressful, to say the least. I know now that traumatic experiences such as this can cause a child to literally shut down and block memories. That's exactly what I did. I shut off that part of my life completely.

My new home was substantially different than the one I had just left. I went from a large two-storey brick home to living in a small travel trailer with no running water. Mom and Dad, newly married, had bought an acre of land and were living in this second-hand travel trailer. While I don't remember the inside, I can still envision the outside of it. It was long and green and parked alongside some trees that protected it from the elements.

The driveway ran along one side of it, and there was lots of space to play. Mom had a small garden behind the trailer. There was an out-house several feet away, which is on the property to this day. It was a far cry from the home where I'd lived to that point, with running water, bathrooms, and separate bedrooms for everyone.

Memories of this time are few, which is typical of young children. However, there are word pictures still in my head. My new dad loved to talk. He was a great storyteller, and I can remember him often telling me about Rattler, a baby red squirrel he'd found. I don't know how Dad caught him, or how long we kept him, but our squirrel lived in a large cage under the trailer. One night it must have rained substantially, because in the morning when Dad got up, Rattler was hanging on from the top of the cage with just his head above water. I remember Dad getting him out of the cage and him scampering up the tree beside our trailer, chittering all the way.

It's said that kids are very resilient, and I would agree, but such resiliency often has a price. The trauma of loss caused by the disruption of leaving my foster parents in my early years remained etched in my psyche for a long time. But I am thankful to my foster parents and to God—I was able to gradually transition into my new life thanks to the secure attachment I'd experienced in those early years. (Regrettably, I was unable to express my gratitude to my foster dad before he passed away.)

My new dad was working as a wheelsman on Great Lake freighters. He would be away from home from April to October, which meant it was just Mom and I together for six months of the year. Not having a dad in the home daily was challenging. Mom did her best but was essentially a single mother much of her life.

Judging from the little I remember, the next couple of years were generally good. Both Mom and Dad shared pleasant stories of those early days. One such story was of me taking a pack of my dad's cigarettes—I was around four at this point. I broke every one of them in half. Mom said I was making a point: *No more smoking, Dad!* I don't remember being punished for that; we just laughed.

Often during my preschool years, when Dad was home from the ships, he would take me to town to buy ice cream, just he and I. I loved spending time with him. By the time I was four, Dad lovingly adopted me.

Dad was a handsome man of 5' 10" with his hair slicked back and a ready smile. He always dressed up to go into town, usually to Smith's Garage, where he'd meet the gang and "shoot the breeze," as he would say, while Mom did the weekly grocery shopping. I think he loved me deeply in those early years. As I got older, Dad taught me to play his favorite game, crokinole. He was hilarious, most often scattering the pieces all over the floor and making us duck for cover. Those were the good times.

However, alcohol changed my dad's demeanor dramatically. Where some drunks become docile and jovial, Dad became violent and aggressive. He became loud, cursing and swearing, throwing anything that was handy. If he was angry with me, he'd slap me hard across the face until my ears rang.

Mom was a pretty, petite 4' 11" brunette, with a great figure and had, as my dad would say, "great legs!" She was full of life and had a happy-go-lucky personality much of the time. But there was another side to her. She would turn on a dime, like flipping a switch, becoming suspicious, accusatory, and angry. I learned quickly to avoid her when she was like this as she became highly unpredictable. I don't remember her hitting me like Dad did, but in some ways, her erratic behaviour was even more frightening.

I think in the early days they were very much in love. But even then, socializing was a problem. Dad's buddies were heavy drinkers, and when Dad was with them, the drinking quickly got out of control. In these situations, it took little to set him off, and you never knew exactly what might trigger the change. Still, he avoided drinking excessively until I was about six. I suspect his drinking became his way of dealing with the marital problems that began to surface.

My dad and grandfather soon built a one-room house for us to live in, as the trailer had seen better days and had never been meant to be a permanent residence. We still had the outhouse, but now we had running water in the farm-style kitchen sink, and a woodstove.

Our new house was not much bigger than what a large bedroom would be today. Mom and Dad had a double bed with a curtain around it, and I slept in a small single bed at the foot of it. It certainly didn't provide them with much privacy! The kitchen boasted an old white porcelain sink. A hand pump which brought water from a shallow dug well beside a small creek that ran alongside the house was attached. This sink stood on a small unfinished wooden box with a curtain that Mom had stretched across the front. Under the sink was where she kept some cleaning supplies as well as a steel dishpan. The few dishes were kept in a small cupboard against the west wall along with canned goods.

A few years later hydro was brought into the house, and an electric range was added. Next to the oven was a round, handmade woodstove which supplied heat during those long Canadian winters. The beds were next to this stove, while on another wall there was a small window beside a tin cupboard. The only door faced south. Above the sink was another small window. There was no indoor plumbing.

There were times when I thought my dad was wonderful, and other times I thought he was crazy. He would have the woodstove going on those cold winter nights. It was great when he put the right amount of wood in, but I remember times when he stuffed it too full and closed all the drafts, and we'd watch the metal on the stovepipes turn red. I was terrified that the stove would blow up or that something would catch fire.

Wood wasn't the only thing Dad would throw into the stove. One night, against Mom's protests, he threw in an aerosol can. The noise was deafening! The door blew off the stove. Remnants of the can and burning wood streamed onto the cement floor. If we had been sitting directly in front of the stove, who knows what the outcome would have been. Mom yelled, Dad swore, and I sat in silence watching the scene unfold. If we'd had wood or carpet flooring, the whole house could have gone up in smoke. As it was, the fire on the floor was quickly quenched as Dad poured a bucket of water on it. All that was left to tell the story was a large black mark on the cement. Dad would tell that story repeatedly to his friends with great relish, laughing it off as a non-event.

An addition to our one-room house was added in 1967 when I was twelve. This extension consisted of a living room, two small bedrooms, a bathroom, and an unfinished basement for storage. Our one-acre property backed onto a treed hillside, which I came to love. It was my refuge. I loved the outdoors and spent most of my time there when not at school.

I have some great memories of my dad teaching me how to shoot cans off of a huge rock that backed into the hillside. I loved shooting, and still do to this day. I'd help my dad collect fallen brush and build bonfires to burn our household paper. Those fires were stoked 'til the flames were eight feet high. As with the woodstove, Dad was apt to throw anything he had handy onto the bonfire, so it was not unusual to see shrapnel-like objects fly through the air as they snapped and burned. Again, it was simply a miracle that we never got hurt.

When Dad was home, he always had the record player going. He loved country and western music. When he was drunk, he would play the same record most of the night, lifting the needle, starting it over and over again. For years I had those songs rolling around in my head. Whenever I hear them now, it brings back many memories—mostly good memories. Somehow I managed to block out most of the negative ones.

I remember a story often told in Dad's family. One night, Mom and he went to a party at his brother's place. Of course, the men were drinking heavily—ran in the family!—and Dad had taken a few records with him. His brother lived right on the lakeshore, so the music could be heard across the bay for miles.

One of his brothers played the fiddle, one friend a guitar, another a harmonica, someone else the spoons. Everyone was having a great time. The party broke up after midnight, but Dad stayed up playing records. In those days, everyone was invited to a party, including the kids. It was usually the time to meet relatives and neighbours. Most left when the party wound down around one a.m., but Dad would often stay the night. He continued playing one song, lifting the needle on the wax and vinyl record, placing it squarely at the beginning of the song—over and over again. I never learned the name of the song, but at about three in the morning, his sister-in-law came downstairs. She grabbed the record off the player, opened the door, and skipped it across the moonlit water!

Dad told this story frequently. He was angry with her for many years, but it didn't seem to stop him from hanging out and drinking with his siblings and cousins.

There are a couple of memories that stand out from my teen years as well. I was thirteen and raising a pet racoon. Our dog had killed its mother and eight babies, but Dad was able to rescue one baby. He became my pet, and we called him Gomer. Amazingly, Dad had no problem letting me keep him—and what a hoot this comical little guy was!

We had a creek that ran about twenty yards from the house. It was Gomer's favourite place as he grew. Racoons—or "coons" at the time—are the most amazing creatures. Their little black paws are like hands that grip, tear, and wash their food. Gomer's favourite food was the crawfish he'd catch in the creek, and his favourite place to eat these succulent morsels was on the steps between our kitchen and living room. If he could sneak into the house, he'd relax with his meal and leave the shell pieces on the stairs for some innocent person to step on.

The thing about coons is that they are incredibly curious. Gomer, like most coons, seemed to have a propensity for getting into trouble. One summer afternoon, Dad's friend Fred came over. We had a wooden picnic table outside the house. Dad and Fred were enjoying a beer while shooting the breeze. Next thing I saw was Gomer hopping up on the seat and then onto the table. By this time he was half grown, weighing about twenty pounds. He sauntered over to Dad and watched the two men for a minute or so, until Dad put down his bottle. As soon as Dad put the bottle down, Gomer picked it up and tried tipping it into his mouth, spilling its contents in the process.

Dad never seemed to get upset with Gomer's antics, so he held the bottom of the bottle up to stabilize it. Gomer proceeded to drink as much as they would give him—the rest of the bottle. Needless to say, Gomer didn't get off the table nearly as confidently as he got on. He walked unsteadily to the edge, fell off, and ambled away with an odd stagger. This sent the two men into fits of laugher. I walked over in disgust, picked up my pet, and put him in his kennel until he sobered up.

Another episode involved my beautiful Rhode Island Red pet rooster. Yes, I seemed to collect peculiar animals. Rooty, as he was known, stayed in my bedroom at night. His home was in a tall ceiling tile box, left over from our house building. Looking back, I can hardly believe my parents put up with this rooster crowing at sunrise. The noise probably only affected Mom, as Dad was usually sleeping off a hangover.

One night Fred, Dad's drinking buddy, was once again visiting. The drinking had commenced and Dad had the record player blaring when Fred suddenly got the bright idea to grab Dad's black lunchbox and some white chalk. He proceeded to draw a horizontal line across the center of the lunchbox. The idea was to hypnotize my bird. There they were, Dad holding the lunchbox, Fred holding the bird. Fred moved Rooty back and forth as the rooster stared at the white line. Then he set him down to watch Rooty totter off, dizzy from the movement. There was a lot of laughter, and no animals were harmed in this prank. But I thought, *What jerks!* I picked up my pet and headed off to my room in a huff.

These were innocent experiences, but Dad was unpredictable. He would get an idea in his head and there was no talking him out of it. His ideas led to the untimely deaths of at least two of my pets. One was a pup named Callie, about six months old, the other a Siamese cat named Taffy.

Callie wasn't home when I returned from school one afternoon, which was unusual. I asked Mom if she knew where Callie was, and she said, "No." I looked high and low for her. She'd never strayed before. I got on my bike and headed up and down the road. No sign of her. I came home at dark, but she hadn't returned.

The next day I hit the road again, riding much farther and checking with neighbours along the way. No Callie. Finally, just before supper, I returned home in tears, exhausted and drained. I don't know where Dad was, but Mom was home when I arrived. She saw how upset I was, so she decided to tell me what had happened. "Your dad shot her."

"What do you mean shot her?" I yelled.

Then the story came out. Apparently Dad got it in his head that Callie, who had been in heat, had gotten pregnant. He decided he didn't want pups. So he took her to the back of the property, shot her, and buried her at the end of the garden.

I was angry and speechless. I don't know who I was most angry with at that moment—Dad for shooting my sweet dog, or Mom for outright lying to me in the first place. I realize now that she thought she was helping, but it only added fuel to the fire of my distrust and disgust in both of them. I believe that it's due to the incredible duplicity I saw in my parents that I became such a truth speaker and seeker. I hate being lied to.

This wasn't the only time, though, that Dad decided to shoot one of my pets. When I was sixteen, I bought a Siamese kitten for twenty-five dollars from my paper route savings. That was a considerable amount to pay for a pet in the seventies, especially in a farming community. I loved this cat. She was personable and very much my cat. She'd follow me everywhere and sit on my lap for hours, purring happily.

Taffy didn't particularly like Dad, and she had a bad habit of wandering through the house or yard crying for me when I was at school. I guess Dad got fed up with listening to her, so he must have followed her out into the yard and then shot her. This time, though, he decided not to bury my pet. He didn't seem to appreciate the impact of his senseless and impulsive act.

4

I got off the bus after school and headed to the house. Dad met me at the door and said, "I killed that yowling cat of yours today. She's out back." I just stared at him with a thousand-yard stare. Up to this point, I had had my share of sadness and loss, but for some reason Taffy's death hit me especially hard. I felt devastated. I had loved her like a best friend. She was more like a faithful dog than a cat. She was mine. I bought her. Cared for her. What right did he have to take away the one thing that brought me so much joy in the midst of this maniacal family?

I turned and walked away in total disgust, angrier than I think I had ever been. The anger didn't dissipate when I saw my beautiful cat lying on the grass behind the house, bullet between her eyes, mouth open, blood oozing out. I sat beside her crying and vowed that I would never forgive him for this. A wall went up around my heart toward my dad, and it was years before I finally chose to forgive him.

Dad's drinking took its toll, and I believe it contributed to the development of Alzheimer's in his late fifties. Before he was diagnosed, he would do crazy things, like ordering my mom to ride on the motorcycle or snowmobile with him when he was drunk. He was a crazy driver. No one liked riding with him in his truck, let alone on a motorcycle or snowmobile. Speed was his best friend. Alzheimer's just exacerbated his foolish driving. Mom often feared for her life under these conditions—and rightfully so—but she was too fearful to say no as Dad would fly off the handle, and she would pay a heavy price.

Dad's condition deteriorated in the last five years of his life and he became very difficult for my mom to contend with. As I lived an hour's drive away and was raising six children by that time, I was very little help. It finally came to the point where we had to hospitalize him. This was a very difficult decision for Mom and me. We had to lie to him to get him into the car. I hate lying and felt guilty for doing this. Regardless of all the other events throughout our lives, institutionalizing Dad was heartbreaking. For much of my life, this was the only dad I could remember, and even with his alcoholic outbursts, I still loved him. For me, the good times will forever balance the bad.

Although my early home life had definite ups and downs and abuse, it was simply a dull shadow compared to what my children experienced.

Both of my parents had been traumatized as children—Mom losing her own mom when she was only five, and Dad being the "outcast" of the family for a reason I will never understand. If they had had the advantages of modern psychotherapy, how much different their lives might have been.

The early years with Mom were generally positive. She was happy and jovial most of the time. She looked at the bright side of everything. She always seemed to be smiling. I remember how she loved baseball and would talk of playing on teams in her teen years. She also loved spending a day skating with her friends in her youth.

She would often pitch a ball to me on the front lawn. Her favorite pastime, though, was playing board games, such as Snakes and Ladders and, later, Monopoly. I couldn't figure out how she always won at Monopoly, and it became a joke years later with my children. They would always catch her cheating, which she fervently denied!

We lived about ten miles from town. Mom didn't have a driver's licence and Dad was away six months of the year, leaving us homebound. I often felt quite lonely and isolated. The closest neighbour was about half a mile away.

I was six and beginning grade 1. I stood at the end of our driveway awaiting the big yellow bus, excited but filled with trepidation for the day ahead. I was excited at the thought of starting school but apprehensive about making friends. I was a very shy child. Nevertheless, off I went, climbing the seemingly enormous steps of the bus and then looking for a place to sit. The bus driver seemed to understand my hesitancy and encouraged me to sit behind him. What a relief. Throughout my school experience, having Denny as the bus driver was the best. After the first few months, I would chat merrily away to him. By the time I was in my teens, I'm sure he was happy to see me sit at the back of the bus!

Although I remember very little of the events of my early childhood, I do know that from the age of six onward, a new fear set in. Mom decided to go to work at the local cabinet-making factory. I was taken to a babysitter after school. The babysitter was married to a man named Peter who had obvious learning difficulties. He was not as tall as my dad, but very thin and wiry, and I knew immediately to stay away from him. One of their two daughters was in my class at school so at least I felt that I had a friend there. These girls also avoided their dad as much as they could, so I did my best to stay out of his way and play with them in their bedroom.

They had a teenage brother, Geoff, who was mentally handicapped. He was devious and crude, and he frightened me horribly. Both he and his dad were physically abusive.

The pervasive memory I have during this time is like a video clip, one I'd like to erase forever. Their mother, who worked with my mom, drove my mother to work and back. I hadn't been going there after school for very long when one day I got off the school bus and Peter was waiting. He grabbed my hand and led me inside. As the other girls raced to their bedroom, he led me upstairs. Geoff was sitting on the bed in the room I was taken to.

I felt overwhelming fear. My heart began to pump rapidly, and I tried to pull away from Peter's tightened grip on my wrist. I had no idea what was going to happen, but even as a child I felt the evil. The atmosphere had changed. It felt charged with something unspeakable. And it was. The look in their eyes, the touch of their hands as they made me take off my clothes, and the palpable terror I felt was paralyzing. The pain was excruciating. I heard myself sobbing and felt the tears flowing down my cheeks as I lay there frozen. I felt like a robot as I agonizingly pushed myself off the bed to put on my clothes. Whenever I think of this time my mind wants to shut down.

It was during one of these incidents that the wife came home from work early. I remember seeing her in the doorway as father and son were assaulting me. Instead of helping me, she simply turned her back and walked out of the room and down the stairs. She never spoke a word about it, and I already knew better than to tell my mom or dad. As I watched her leave the room that day, I felt such desolation and abandonment. In that moment, I hated her. She knew exactly what was happening and she refused to protect me. Even as I write this, I can feel anger starting to well up. She allowed her deviant husband, this creep of a man, and her lascivious son to sexually assault me over the next three years while Mom was working.

Life at home was also changing. It was becoming more and more a place of insecurity and fear. The happy times I had experienced at home in my younger years became few and far between.

I was about nine when Mom suffered a head injury at work. This likely resulted in an undiagnosed concussion. This unfortunate event ended her work at the factory. While it was devastating in many ways, it was a blessing in disguise for me as it meant I no longer had to return to the babysitter. Unfortunately for all of us, Mom refused to see a doctor and things at home began to deteriorate quickly.

Mom's behaviour changed dramatically as she began to experience delusional paranoia. She became suspicious of every vehicle that slowed down on our road, and in the rare occurrence when an ambulance passed by, she would be beside herself thinking it was coming to take her away in a straightjacket.

I had no idea what a straightjacket was, but her fear was tangible and it created silence in our home. Dad and I were afraid to make any sudden moves in case we were accused of signalling the "enemy." Dad had a habit of using his car keys to clean under his fingernails. It's a habit I detested, because Mom would go into a state of panic, claiming that he was signalling the police and/or hospital workers to have her committed. There was no way to calm her down and her hysterics were incredibly disturbing to me.

While we ascribed this behaviour to her head injury, I was to find out in my early forties that Mom had been diagnosed with paranoid schizophrenia at age seventeen. Dad determined that he could no longer work on the ships, so in order to be home at night he took a job at a local military base about three miles away. There were other incidents that took place over the next few years that would leave me confused and anxious.

A particular one comes to mind where we gathered around the kitchen table. Dad and I sat down at the table for dinner. Mom went to the oven and brought a small roasting pan over to the table that she had set nicely for our meal. As no other food was on the table, I was expecting that Mom had cooked a roast of beef or maybe a chicken with carrots, onions, and potatoes. Those were the only things she ever cooked in that pan.

You could have heard a pin drop when the lid was removed. It felt as though the air had been sucked out of the room. There in the pan was my little brown teddy bear looking up at us with its black button eyes. Shock and confusion hardly describe my feelings. How does a nine-year-old deal with such an experience?

I have to say that Dad rescued the moment. He quietly turned to me and asked if I'd like a hotdog. I don't remember Mom's reaction or response at all. In fact, I can see her in my mind. After lifting the lid, she looked at the teddy bear with a blank stare, seemingly unable to interpret what had happened. It was like she was in some other space, not really registering what was happening.

One thing I know is that such incidents happened often over the next few years. This was one time when Dad had not been drinking and therefore was able to handle the incident with grace.

Looking back, I can perhaps understand why Dad may have started to drink heavily. He didn't know how to deal with Mom; and was unhappy in his new job, and I believe he drank in an attempt to alleviate his own pain and confusion. Of course, this escalated the tension at home and the cycle of emotional and physical abuse began. As I mentioned earlier, some people become mellower when they drink, but alcohol affected my father in a totally destructive manner.

I believe that Dad's inability to understand and deal with my mom's departures from reality led him to a greater dependence on alcohol, making our life more fearful. He began lashing out at anything that displeased him, and Mom was the most constant source of his displeasure.

Mom hated his drunkenness; it turned him into a different man. Dad's escalating unpredictable behaviour combined with Mom's paranoia made a disastrous duo. Dad and I became hypervigilant in our attempt to avoid upsetting Mom. Mom and I, on the other hand, walked on eggshells whenever Dad was drinking. Frequently Mom would pour full bottles of liquor down the sink. Of course, this simply stoked the fires of adversity. It seemed like a never-ending wheel we were on, kind of like being a hamster in a spinning ball.

While living in the one-room home of about 250 square feet, Mom decided that the cement floor needed to be painted. I arrived home from school earlier than Dad. The moment he opened the door, we knew he'd been drinking. He took one look at the wet floor and flew into a rage. Mom was down on her hands and knees painting when he belligerently declared there was no way he was going to walk around the wet paint. Wearing his army combat boots, he forcefully pushed her down and began to brutally stomp on her small body. He then reached down and commenced to push her head against the hard floor and viciously swirled her hair into the wet paint.

Dad's aggression didn't stop there. On several occasions, he yanked the telephone cord from the wall—there were no cordless or cellular phones in those days—angrily throwing the phone through the kitchen window. Throwing the phone out the window was a common event. I have no idea how many windowpanes had to be replaced. It was probably a good thing that there were only two windows in the small house. Many times I remember going out and there would be the phone hanging by its cord from a branch on the nearby tree.

On this particular night, the wet-paint-on-the-floor night, hearing the commotion, I remember bolting to the door, taking in the appalling scene before me, standing there frozen with my heart pounding in fear. I was struggling to understand what was transpiring before my eyes, when Mom pleaded, "Get help!"

I whirled about and bolted out the door and down the road to our next-door neighbour's house, about a quarter of a mile away. It was pitch-dark outside and I had not donned a coat or put shoes on my bare feet. The temperature was hovering around the freezing mark and I can clearly remember running frantically through freezing cold puddles.

I was in hysterics by the time I arrived at the neighbour's. I told her that I needed her to come over to our house because my dad was killing my mom. To my dismay, she casually informed me that she'd be along shortly, and then sat down to finish her cigarette.

I was dumbfounded that she was reacting to my obvious anguish so nonchalantly. Even though I stood there before her dishevelled and trembling with cold and fear, she displayed no sense of urgency. Apparently she didn't put much stock in what I was telling her.

I turned and ran back home as quickly as I could, only to find Dad drunkenly slouched at the table and Mom gone. She had gone to lie on the bed. I sat down on my bed, with a wary eye on Dad and the door.

The neighbour arrived sometime later, sat down, and poured each of them a drink. *After what I told you, you're pouring him a drink? Really?* I can still recall the utter disgust I felt for her in that moment. She had betrayed the trust I placed in her. It was bizarre. Dad and she talked and laughed like nothing was awry. The scene was surreal. A short while later, she got up and went home. The police were never called, not then or ever. And, because Dad seemed to have been shielded by others, he had no incentive to curb his violence and aggression. Things just kept getting worse.

My relationship with my parents, already tense and frayed, took a nosedive. I tried to engage with one or the other, whenever an opportunity presented itself, but to little avail. I became more and more withdrawn, spending as much time out of their presence as possible, a difficult task in a one-room house. Schoolwork and books became my focus, my refuge. Even though my mother seemed to recover her mental stability over the next four years, these were difficult and frightful times.

Dad began a new job working as a wheelsman on a ferry. It was only two hours from home, but he worked four hours on, four hours off, so unless he got a shore leave, he didn't come home from the first of May until mid-October.

Dad had begun wheeling freighters on the St. Lawrence when he was only sixteen, after spending his earlier years helping his dad with the family fishing business. Now he worked on a ferry, transporting cars and passengers from the peninsula to the mainland. It was a busy job, as tourists clamoured to get to their cottages or holiday venues, or used the route as a shortcut to the west, heading out on the Trans-Canada Highway.

Dad had his good sides. He loved people and loved to talk and tell stories. That was where he shone. While working aboard ship, my dad never touched a drop of alcohol. Everyone liked him. There he had a place, a position of trust and responsibility. He loved his job.

Dad died when he was only sixty-seven, but I always felt privileged to be there in his dying moments, reading Psalm 23 to him, as Mom and I held his hands. He had changed much in the last years of his life after trusting in Christ as his Saviour. I am forever grateful for those last few years.

5

A Port in the Storm

When I was twelve, Dad and Mom, with the help of Grandpa, my dad's father, decided to build an addition to our one-room dwelling. During that summer I got to work on the house as well. My main job was putting the pink, scratchy insulation between the two-by-fours. Getting the itchy remnants off my skin and out of my clothes at the end of a hot, sticky day was a chore. The pain was definitely worth the gain, as by early fall, my parents and I had our own bedrooms, a bathroom, and a living room. Finally, I had my very own space, my retreat for the next five years, a place where I could drown out the screaming, the yelling, and the threat of violence. I escaped under the covers.

The next year my mom joined Dad working on the ferry. She worked cleaning and in the kitchen over the next two summers, so I needed a place to stay where I could still catch the bus for school before summer break. Grandpa's it was! I was thrilled.

Grandpa was like a port in a storm. He was quiet, thoughtful, kind, and loved having me around—a new experience for me. Grandpa, just past eighty years old, had been a fisherman and boat builder all of his life, and I loved watching him as he worked on the eighteen-foot wooden speedboat he kept in the old shed on the property. He didn't talk a lot, which was fine with me. I would sit on a stool and watch him plane the wood and then finish it with a high-gloss coat to protect it from the elements. His boats were works of art, well-known not only in the surrounding area, but also internationally.

Once school was out, I could help Grandpa look after his three milk cows, letting them out in the morning to pasture on the hill through the day. His favourite was an old girl named Betsy. At the end of the day we'd yell, "Co-boss," and up they'd come. Grandpa kept some laying hens and a few meat birds as well, but it was his raspberry patch that drew locals. Mind you, if you didn't wear long sleeves, picking those raspberries meant lots of cuts on your hands and arms.

I had afternoons to wander on my own and would usually head down the hill to walk about a mile to my cousin's house, situated right on the water. These were third cousins on my dad's side. How I loved it there, swimming and sunning all afternoon, till Grandpa rang the big school bell that hung on his barn. Then up I'd head for supper. In the evening Grandpa would sit in his recliner with Petey, his budgie, sitting on his shoulder and pulling on the few stray hairs he still had left on his head.

This was one of the best years of my life. I felt secure, happy, and loved. How often I wished I could have lived there permanently. Never underestimate the importance of grandparents! Sadly, that winter, Grandpa died. My heart was broken. Looking back now, I realize what a privilege it had been for me to spend his last summer with him.

The next summer I was sent to live with Dad's oldest sister and her husband. I loved them as well, but sorely missed my friends at the bay. I would work in the garden with my aunt or putter around the yard with the chickens, cats, and dog. I made new friends with whom I could bike up and down the country road.

Sometimes I'd be gone for hours. In those days, personal safety was not really a concern; no one worried about fourteen-year-old girls being kidnapped. I was diligent to return on time, so as not to worry my aunt.

During my teen years, alcohol addiction took over Dad's life. He attempted to numb his inner pain and sorrows from the pressures of life. He would drink every last drop of beer or whiskey in the house and then, in desperation, he would proceed to imbibe rubbing alcohol. This often made him desperately ill, but he never learned. Mom would go around and clean up after him. I resented her for that. I often told her that Dad should clean up his own "stinking vomit."

Dad ended up with bleeding ulcers and in tremendous pain. I remember him often spitting up blood. He was put on medication. Surgery was suggested, but he stubbornly ignored the advice and continued to drink. Life devolved into a sad and fear-filled cycle.

One of Dad's favourite pastimes when drinking was to hop in the car and go for a drive, usually ending up at a friend's house. Mom regularly hid his car keys because she was terrified that he'd kill either himself or someone else. Fortunately this never happened, but he did frighten a lot of people.

Mom became more confrontational over the years and began to challenge Dad's drinking. She would dump full bottles of whiskey or rye down the sink. This infuriated Dad. He was livid.

Things progressively deteriorated and reached a climax one night in 1972. Most nights the drinking and yelling seemed to go on forever. I would hide deep under the covers, cowering in fear, hoping and praying that I didn't wake in the morning to broken windows, broken furniture, or worse. I would usually let the scene play out, as most often it was just a screaming match rather than a physical altercation. But this night I decided to step between them and defend Mom.

Dad saw that as a challenge to his authority. He erupted, pushing me into the coatrack by the front door. I fell against the wall, coats and hangers clattering around my head. Dad grabbed one of the hangers that was now wrapped around my neck and started pulling on it.

I don't remember what happened next. Perhaps Dad realized what he was doing and released me, or perhaps Mom shoved him aside. I can't remember. However it came about, Mom and I quickly beat it out through the open door and stayed at a neighbour's that night.

The next morning, when we arrived home, we were shocked to learn that Dad had planned to shoot us. He sat all night with a shotgun across his lap, waiting for the door to open to blow us away. Around three a.m., one of his drinking buddies showed up. Luckily for his friend, Dad had fallen asleep. His friend pushed opened the front door, as it was never locked, and surprised my dad. Dad didn't have time to lift the gun and shoot, or else this friend could easily have been killed.

This event pushed me over the edge. I left home to live about forty-five minutes away, taking a job as a live-in nanny. Leaving home came with a high price emotionally; I was overwhelmed with guilt and worry. Mom was now on her own. How could I do this to her? What would happen? What if Dad killed her? I weighed this painful decision for several months before I finally made the choice to leave.

My turbulent childhood was but a prelude for what was to come in my adult life.

6

The year was 1972. It was the year Richard Nixon, president of the United States, ordered the development of a space shuttle program and the Soviet Union sent an unmanned spacecraft named Spaceship Luna 20 to land on the moon. The Vietnam war continued amidst anti-war protests. The Watergate scandal surfaced in the U.S., and the first Gay Pride march happened in London, England, the movement having had its beginnings in the U.S.

And in Canada? In Canadian politics, Pierre Elliot Trudeau, prime minister since 1967, was elected again by a slim margin. The real news of the day was that September 28, 1972, was dubbed "the Greatest Day in Canadian History." It was the day a hockey game—the good ol' hockey game—gave a nation the thrill of its lifetime. Team Canada's victory over the Soviet Union's national hockey team is one of the most celebrated moments in the country's sports history. Many Canadians of that generation remember precisely where they were when Paul Henderson scored his famous game-winning goal.

It was December and I had just turned seventeen. Politics and sports were the farthest things from my mind. It was the time of polyester suits, choirboy dresses, miniskirts, crushed velvet, and bellbottom pants. I was in grade 11 and had just begun dating a guy a few years older than me. I'd known Chuck since I was a child.

We'd attended the same family reunions, and his family had come to visit several times.

Our moms were friends. My dad was an uncle to Chuck's mother. I realize that's a bit confusing. My adoptive dad was the second youngest in a family of eight. His sister, Janet, who was the second oldest of the family by eighteen years, was Chuck's grandmother.

Janet's daughter, Joyce, was just a few years younger than my dad, about the same age as my mom. Joyce was Chuck's mom. This may be as clear as mud, but these are the facts. All my cousins on Dad's side were several years older than me, many of them married with their own children. As you can see, Chuck and his four siblings are my second cousins (via adoption).

With Chuck now on the scene, Dad decided it was time to give me the information I'd been long awaiting. At seventeen, I would finally have the discussiosn the nine-year-old had craved. *"It doesn't matter. We can talk about this when you are older."* The confusing veil was about to be lifted.

Dad wasn't drinking that day, which was something unusual. With my mother absent and melancholy written on his face, Dad unexpectedly and cautiously explained our family history. He said, "You know, I'm not your real dad." Words I'd heard before. I felt relieved on the one hand, but on the other, I was thinking, *Well, gee, Dad, I've been waiting for this conversation for eight years!*

Dad, his heart breaking, informed me, "Your mom was raped and you are the result of that rape. Because of your mother's circumstance and illness, you were placed in foster care." My head was spinning, but something resonated in me. Suddenly, at seventeen, the void I'd lived with was being filled. Yet questions swirled. *What are you talking about? Another family? I don't remember.*

Dad continued, "After your mom and I married, we brought you home to live with us. I adopted you as my own."

I was in a fog. I had no memory of this. I was trying to make sense of it, but it was difficult to process. I wanted to shut my mind off. This was out of left field. *Okay, yes, he told me years ago that I wasn't his, but I was too young to really understand what that meant.*

At nine, I thought that I had lived with Mom until she married Dad. Everything had been hush-hush. Don't talk about this or that. In fact, very little "family business" was ever discussed—at least with me.

Now I had another family? Why couldn't I remember this? I'm yelling internally to myself, *Think, think, think!* Nope, nothing. I just stared at him. Once again, my emotions were in turmoil, but even worse, this inner knowledge conflicted me. This was not sitting well with this seventeen-year-old! Why couldn't we have talked about this before?

I felt angry and overwhelmed. My questioning took a turn. "Dad, who were they? Where do they live? Can we see them?"

Dad clammed up. "I've probably already told you too much. You need to talk with your mother."

"Please tell me, Dad."

"No. You'll have to talk to your mother," he repeated.

Great! I already know what that will be like. As easy as getting blood from a stone! And that's exactly what it was like. When I went to talk to Mom, she looked pale and simply stated, "They were a good family. I don't want to talk about it." That's exactly how it was left.

That's how things were dealt with in the family. But I wanted to talk about it.

Over the next several years, I would glean pieces of information here and there from relatives, but my parents revealed nothing more. No one knew who my foster parents were, and Mom wasn't talking.

I now realize that I was part of a special club—the 1% club. These are children conceived and born as a result of their mother being raped. Yes, I am definitely "pro-birth" and "pro-life." My mother was offered an abortion, which I am thankful she rejected.

7

Young, Naïve, & Gullible

As a child, my dream was to become a teacher. I was an industrious student, far more than most of my peers. It was in books and learning that I found solace. I related to adults far better than to peers, as I spent so much time with them. But my hopes and dreams of being a teacher evaporated during the high school years, as the physical and emotional abuse intensified. My dream ended when I left school after grade 11. Although I loved school, higher learning had never been a priority in our household. My mom had only gone as far as grade 9, and Dad finished grade 8.

Soon after leaving home, I got a summer job as a nanny. Shortly thereafter, I managed to get a more permanent position with a manufacturing company. I loved working and having my own paycheck. I'd had a paper route since I was twelve, but the money I earned had mostly gone to my dad. Now I felt a liberating sense of freedom and autonomy. Being my own person, paying my bills, and being a contributing member of society was fulfilling.

To suggest that, at seventeen, I was young and naïve would have been an understatement. I had a strongly developed sense of morality, especially when it came to sex. However, I had been influenced by those around me and took up smoking and drinking.

Remember Chuck? I'd started dating him about six months before

I left home. Chuck's interest in me served to help raise my self-confidence and my level of "acceptability" at school. His quiet demeanour and his kindness elevated my sense of worth. Once I'd left home, Chuck and I lived closer to one another, allowing us to see each other more regularly.

Dating Chuck was exciting. He treated me well, taking me for dinner and to the movies. And, like me, he loved hiking and the outdoors. I was in love. I'd never had anyone who wanted to spend time with me, and I drank in every moment we were together.

Dating in the seventies was a far cry from what it is today. Many of my peers were still virgins when they married, even though they lived through the sixties sexual revolution. As for Chuck and me, most of our initial dates were centered round his family activities. I enjoyed the company of his siblings, as they were of a similar age.

We had been dating for a while when Chuck began pressuring me for sex. He did not share my desire to wait until marriage. I was unhappy about it, but he was persistent, telling me that if I didn't "put out" he'd quit dating me. He'd been telling me for some time that he loved me, but now that love came with conditions. I was hurt. Our relationship came down to an ultimatum.

I knew little of personal boundaries. My childhood insecurities resurfaced, and the pervasive thoughts that no one else would ever love me convinced me that I really had no choice.

There had been many warning signs earlier in our relationship that pointed to Chuck's hostility, immaturity, and lack of responsibility. He proved to be lazy and, as I discovered later, once married, he was repeatedly unfaithful. But because of my own low self-esteem, I simply ignored the signs.

One time while we were dating, I was visiting his family for Sunday dinner. Dinner at his house was always an event for my taste buds. His mom was a marvelous cook and served mouth-watering desserts.

This particular night, Chuck and his brother got into an argument. I have no idea now what it was about, but I remember thinking, *How trivial.* Without warning, Chuck picked up a knife and hurled it at his younger brother, barely missing his head. Fortunately, his brother ducked and avoided injury.

I was appalled. This was something to be expected in my childhood home, but here it seemed incongruent. In my estimation, Chuck at twenty-two should have shown more self-control. I left the table, put on my coat, and started walking home. I had walked a couple of miles when Chuck drove up, beseeching me to get into the car. Had I had more wisdom at the time, I would have walked the rest of the way, washing my hands of the relationship.

A short time thereafter, Chuck took me to the local bar that we frequented. We met up with his cousin and her boyfriend for a night of drinking. My apartment was a short walk from the bar, so we all went back there to spend the night. I had no idea where this night would lead.

Having had too much to drink, my resistance was low as we started to make out on the couch. I soon found myself under him on the floor, right next to his cousin and her boyfriend. I remember Chuck kissing me and saying, "Let's switch!" That was a road too far for me. I sobered up quickly. What he was suggesting disgusted me. I should have sex with this other man? And the woman was his cousin? Chuck was eager to have sex with his cousin! I was appalled just lying next to them, and to think that he now wanted to press it further made me physically ill. I jumped up and headed for the bathroom.

That sure dampened the atmosphere. Everyone soon left. I was once again on my own and grateful for it. I'm thankful that I resisted his deviant appetite. But if I'd only had the fortitude to tell him to never come back, my life would most likely have taken a very different route.

Three days before my eighteenth birthday I decided to attend a church service, something I'd only done as a child with my aunt and uncle. It was a day that changed the trajectory of my life. In that service, I found a peace that I had never known. At the end of the service I responded to the altar call, went to the front, and gave my life to Christ.

I decided then and there that I would attempt to live my life in accordance with biblical principles. I stopped smoking and drinking. My decision put pressure on my relationship with Chuck, but he assured me that he had made a commitment to follow Christ as well. We began to attend church services together, although his behaviour unfortunately remained unchanged. Again, I ignored the warning signs.

As a new Jesus follower, I wanted to believe the best in everyone. I made excuses for Chuck's lack of employment, his indiscretions and manipulation. I felt that forgiveness for his past transgressions was the best route. Unfortunately, I had a lot to learn about what forgiveness was and was not. Lacking personal boundaries, I was definitely vulnerable to manipulation and coercion, couched as it was in the words of love.

Over the next few months, Chuck would often drop in at a local hair salon. He claimed it was to visit with an older friend who worked there. Chuck was in no hurry to introduce us, which surprised me, but I sluffed it off. It was round this time that Chuck proposed to me, and at the ripe old age of eighteen, I accepted his proposal. In hindsight, I realize how foolish and desperate I was for love. But it gets worse.

To my shock, during the engagement Chuck told me the truth about his relationship with the man at the hair salon. They were involved in a homosexual relationship, but he assured me that he was quitting the relationship. Chuck claimed to be committed only to me. In blind faith, I believed him.

Chuck and I soon began making plans for our wedding. It would be relatively simple. Finances were an issue, as Chuck was once again unemployed. He still lived at home, neither paying rent nor contributing to expenses—more red lights ignored. Looking back, I'm overcome with sadness for the teenager who didn't know how to stand her ground. I realize now how very good Chuck was at manipulating others to get what he wanted.

8

Proceed with Caution!

Although I was working full time, my income was just above minimum wage and planning a wedding was expensive. Paying my rent along with other living expenses used up most of my money. A new wedding dress was out of the question, so I borrowed one from a friend who had recently wed. My future mother-in-law and the church ladies helped prepare a reception meal, while my mom and dad contributed by paying for a dance at a local community center. I was grateful for all their help.

As my dad and I drove to the church on the day of my wedding, he looked over at me and said, "Do you want to call it off?" I was shocked by his candor. My dad and I rarely talked, and he certainly had said nothing for or against the upcoming marriage. I looked over at him and wished he had spoken to me months earlier. If we had had a good father-daughter relationship, I would have told him so much about my concerns. I could have discussed Chuck's behaviour with him, and perhaps I would have been equipped to leave the relationship.

Throughout my childhood, Dad when he was drinking had called me ugly and stupid. These words probably hurt me more than anything else. I was left thinking, *Who would ever love me? I'm ugly, stupid, and unlovable.* I clung to Chuck's proclamation of love like a lifeline. In fact, looking back, I was desperate to hold on to the one person who told me he loved me. I had never heard those words from either Mom or Dad.

I had longed for a better relationship with Dad and now for the first time he was actually reaching out. I really wanted to say, *Yes! Call it off.* In my heart I knew there was something amiss. Unfortunately, I wasn't strong enough to say no and stop the ceremony that was taking place in a half hour. How could I let my family and friends down like that? I sat in stunned silence thinking about Dad's comments. *I can't call off the wedding, everyone is waiting.*

To maintain a pseudo peace at home and a warm relationship with Chuck, I felt compelled to please others. "No, it's okay," I responded. Only later would I realize that it was never to be "okay."

9

Forever & Ever?

The wedding was over. It didn't take long for life to settle into a routine. I loved being married. I felt a sense of security and belonging. A place to call home, shared with the person I loved.

I tried hard to please Chuck. He was the oldest of a family of five and in his earlier years had often helped his mom in the kitchen. He knew how to cook, whereas I had never learned. Mom taught me very little about cooking. So I embarked on a steep learning curve. After work and on weekends, dinner recipes became my reading materials. I got the hang of casseroles and roast beef meals pretty quickly. My next attempt was to make pies. This was a whole other story that quickly exposed some of Chuck's true nature.

Chuck's mom was an excellent baker and pies were her speciality. Back to the recipe book—after all, how hard could it be, or so I thought! I'll never forget my first pie. It was apple, and I was so proud of how good it looked. It smelled delicious as the aroma of cinnamon and nutmeg filled the air. I was excited about what I had accomplished. I cut the first piece, dished it up, and served it to my husband.

He took one bite, picked up the plate, and threw it at me. I was standing in our kitchen getting my own slice when the plate flew past my head and hit the refrigerator. I was stunned. I stood there looking at the mess, him yelling something about the hard-as-nails crust. He opened the door and walked out of the apartment, slamming the door behind him. I stood there in shock. He had never treated me like this before.

Tears fell as I cleaned up the mess. I thought about Chuck's actions and about my dad. Dad had often thrown and broken things— although never did he complain about Mom's cooking—but he'd only been aggressive and violent when he was drinking. That had always been my fallback excuse for Dad's aggressive behaviour. Chuck, on the other hand, hadn't had anything to drink. In his rage, he was acting like a spoiled child, I thought. My response was predictable. I just needed to do better.

I decided to talk with Chuck's mom and a lady at the church who offered to help me learn the art of making pies. I didn't discuss Chuck's behaviour with them or anyone else. I believed that he had become enraged because I was so inept, and if I could only do it right, he would be pleased and everything would be okay. This became the mantra I lived by: *I have to do better*. With practice, my baking improved and I managed to keep his stomach full in the hopes of avoiding any further altercations.

A month after this incident, Chuck had an appointment with an urologist. He hadn't been sick or complained of any pain, but when I questioned him about it, he was vague on details. The reason for said appointment was never made clear to me. When he returned, he explained that the doctor had told him that we should try to have children as soon as possible, because apparently it was unlikely that Chuck would ever father children. I really didn't know what to make of this. I didn't ask him about the doctor's diagnosis, nor did I question Chuck's motives. I accepted what he said as truth. To my knowledge, he never went for a follow-up appointment, and looking back, I believe it was a ruse to get me to agree to have children immediately.

I was nineteen and had no intention of having children until at least my mid-twenties. I really wanted to wait a few years as I was so young and immature, and we really needed to get some savings together. But now I felt pressured to begin a family. If getting pregnant at such a young age would prevent the disappointment of not being able to conceive later in life, as he claimed, I was on board with it. Had it occurred to me that he was lying, I would never have agreed.

Two months later, I was pregnant. I guess that doctor had misdiagnosed Chuck's condition. What a surprise! During my pregnancy, we moved closer to our parents, renting a small house on the shore of Georgian Bay. Chuck finally landed a job at a local foundry and we were making a little headway financially. At least we were able to pay our bills and buy some furniture.

Before getting this new job and by month's end, Chuck had most often been strapped for cash. He'd often go to his father and ask for money. Chuck's parents were barely able to provide for their own family, yet his dad always seemed to find a way to help Chuck out. This was embarrassing to me, as I had never gone to my parents for money—or anything, for that matter. They'd taught me personal responsibility, and so I was appalled that Chuck continually borrowed money but seldom returned it.

I loved living on the waterfront. My happiest times as a child had been on these shores, and now, here I was again. A couple days prior to my due date, I had a craving for a fish dinner and so decided I would go fishing. We owned a small fourteen-foot aluminum motorboat that we docked out front. It was a beautiful sunny day, so I grabbed the tackle and a life jacket and headed out. I got the outboard started, but I was hardly past the end of the long dock before the motor sputtered and died.

I tried and tried to restart the engine, but to no avail. As I looked up, I realized that the wind had picked up and changed direction. It was now what is called an offshore wind, meaning the waves were pushing my boat farther out into the bay. Sudden wind changes were not an unusual event on the bay, as storms tended to come up quickly. Realizing that I wouldn't be able to start the motor, I grabbed the oars and started rowing, but with little success. The wind was picking up and waves were beginning to splash over the hull. Terrified, all I could think about was washing up on some unknown shore and having this baby in the bottom of the boat.

If I was to avoid ending up on one of the uninhabited islands across the bay, I had to get the attention of cottagers. I took off my life jacket, stood up in the boat, and began to wave it. Yep! That's what I did. Looking back, I can hardly believe that I didn't capsize. I could see dark clouds rolling in and whitecaps beginning to form on the waves—never a good sign. I knew that I would be in danger if I continued drifting out into the middle of the bay.

I figured that I might be better off attempting to swim back to shore rather than continuing to drift out farther. Looking back, I wasn't being particularly rational. There I was, an extremely large nine-months-pregnant woman, standing in a rocking boat, trying to keep my balance, waving a life jacket. It must have been quite a sight, and it's a miracle that I didn't end up overboard. A cell phone would have been handy back then to document my predicament.

I made a promise to God then and there: *Get me out of this mess and I will never turn my back on you.* In spite of my efforts madly paddling, standing and waving, then paddling some more, I kept drifting farther from shore. I had no idea whether anyone had seen me. It was a good thing that I'd spent much of my life around water with my dad and grandpa, or else, in my condition, I might have died of fright.

After about an hour I looked up and to my relief saw a large boat speeding toward me. As it drew alongside, I remember thinking, *What a huge and beautiful yacht this is.* Compared to my little boat, this thing was massive and beautifully decked out.

From about eight feet above me, I was thrown a rope to secure my little boat against the yacht. Given the waves, it would have been too dangerous to tow the boat to shore with me in it. Their concern was how to get this pregnant woman from her skiff to their deck safely. The guys decided that I could be best lifted up backward, and so I was rather ungracefully hauled aboard. If I hadn't been so scared, I would have laughed till I cried. It must have been some sight!

I was later told that an emergency call had come in, but because the local coast guard ship was usually docked in the harbour at the other end of the bay, about sixty nautical miles away, the only ship available was this one—the mayor's yacht. Fortunately, firefighters were close at hand to assist in my rescue. Had there been cell phones back then and had someone taken a video of my rescue, it would likely have gone viral. While it wasn't funny at the time, being able to see it on video today would probably elicit some laughter. I was embarrassed but grateful. We arrived at the marina just before the fury of the storm hit.

Later that night I discovered why the motor stalled. My father-in-law, after returning from fishing the night before, had shut off the gas line valve. It never crossed my mind to check such things, but believe me, I check such things now! Live and learn.

10

The First Born

You'd think that with all the excitement of the boating incident, the baby I was joyously awaiting would make his appearance pretty quickly, but no such luck. Instead, a full three weeks after the due date, my first son was born. He caused quite a stir and excitement, something he continues to do to this day. His entry into the world couldn't be normal; it had to have some flair.

Delivery was imminent when the doctor declared that the umbilical cord was tangled around the baby's neck. He yelled, "Don't push!" It was all I could do to stop pushing. Only pregnant women can appreciate how difficult it can be to stop pushing when a baby decides it wants to come out. As soon as the doctor had untangled the umbilical cord, Garnet was born. But instead of being a nice pink, he was an ashen grey. *Is he going to live?*

As was the custom, the doctor smacked my baby boy on the bottom, and seconds later, I was thrilled to hear his hearty cry. Garnet weighed nine pounds and three ounces and suffered no ill effects from oxygen deprivation. I was so grateful. There is nothing that anyone can say that prepares one for childbirth. Each experience is different, but nothing exceeds the joy of holding your child in your arms. I was in love! Growing up without siblings created a deep longing within me. I had always wanted a brother. Now I had a beautiful baby boy. He was mine to love, cherish, and protect.

We didn't get much time to settle into life with our baby before my husband decided we should move again. Within a month of Garnet's birth, we packed up and moved from our lovely house on the bay to the city that Chuck had grown up in. The only people I knew there were Chuck's sister and one of his aunts.

Garnet was only four months old when I found a job working nights at a nearby cookie factory. Chuck's sister Ruth would sleep at our place overnight to babysit Garnet. I'd return home in the morning to be with him for the day. As it is for most moms, sleep deprivation in the earliest months of my baby's life was common.

One morning when I came home, Ruth proudly showed me how she had finished the laundry the night before, making sure to include Garnet's diapers. I was thrilled—until I took a closer look. A little bleach works well, but too much disintegrates the material! The new diapers were in threads. I was no longer thrilled—but we laughed about it for years. I was barely twenty and Ruth just seventeen, so we both had a lot to learn.

Chuck had grown up with siblings, changing diapers and helping at home, so I followed his lead when it came to child care. Chuck didn't like his sleep disturbed, so Ruth and I did our best to make sure Garnet was as quiet as possible. Keeping Chuck happy was important, and I tried to comply with his wishes. I wanted to be a good wife and mother. While he helped with the housework, he was a demanding perfectionist. He was difficult to please.

One time when Garnet was only about four months old, he became extremely constipated. I expected that this was likely due to the change in his feeding regimen, going from mother's milk to a bottle. As I later learned, this is quite common.

Instead of taking Garnet to the doctor to get medical help, Chuck informed me that it was important that children be given regular enemas (constipated or not). What did I know? Chuck started giving regular enemas to our son. I assumed he knew what he was talking about. Interestingly, though, he did not keep up this practice with our other children.

It wasn't until decades later, after my children began talking about their abuse at the hands of their father that I read about the phenomenon of klismaphilia. This term refers to a sexual condition in which the individual wishes to use enemas for pleasure. A light went on! Chuck wanted to give enemas to his children, not for health reasons, but rather to fuel his sexual desires.

Forty years later my son shared with my current husband and me how his biological father had abused him in this manner. When I explained to my son the phenomenon of klismaphilia and what it meant, he reacted with physical revulsion, doubling over, wailing and heaving. It brought back terrifying moments. But this was only one form of abuse he had suffered and only the tip of the iceberg of Chuck's deviant behaviour. Unfortunately, I was unaware of these hidden horrors.

Our baby was nearly a year old when Chuck and I decided to move to the west coast of Canada. Some friends were moving to Vancouver to go to a Bible college, and Chuck thought he'd like to go as well. I was fine with the idea. I thought it would be a good move for Chuck. I packed up essentials and we hit the road—the third move in our first year of marriage. It must have been hard for our parents to say goodbye to their first grandchild. We celebrated Garnet's first birthday at a Chinese restaurant in Moosejaw, Saskatchewan.

Days of driving were long and tiresome, but Garnet was such a good baby, full of joy and laughter. Back then car seats had been only newly introduced, and laws surrounding them weren't yet strictly enforced. I'd often sit Garnet on my knee, contentedly counting cows with him and watching the scenery go by.

I was so completely in love with my family. I was happy to go wherever Chuck led. Not only that, but I was truly glad at the thought of him pursuing a "godly" life and calling. We would be leaving his past behind and beginning a new life on the west coast.

11

Moving West

Vancouver could very well be one of the most beautiful places in the world to live. At least that's how it seemed to me when we arrived there in 1976. Life seemed full of promise and wonder.

I loved country music, a throwback to my dad's obsessive listening to the great hits of the seventies. Who could ever forget silly songs like "Tennessee Bird Walk" or classic hits like "Coal Miner's Daughter"? But the one that sticks most in my mind was one penned by Donna Fargo, called "Funny Face."

Chuck particularly liked this song and would regularly call me "funny face" as he hummed along. I loved the upbeat melody and truly believed that the words of the song described how he felt about me, that his whole world was wrapped up in me. I certainly felt that way toward him. Not only that, but "funny face" seemed to play well into my own false self-perception.

Chuck enrolled in Bible College and we joined the church associated with it. I loved it there. I met lots of other young people, although I was the only twenty-year-old married with a baby. I found it more comfortable amongst the married-with-children crowd. I saw a bright future for us here, but soon Chuck's sexual addictions began to be exposed.

We'd been in Vancouver for less than a year when Chuck disclosed that he had had a homosexual affair. He said it was just a quick

thing and it was over—would I please forgive him. If he hadn't told me, I would never have known about it. But, because he told me, I thought he was truly repentant and I needed to forgive him. I hid my pain and forgave him. I told no one about it. It was over, and I would carry on with life as usual—so I thought.

I got a job as the receptionist at the church we attended, which meant we had access to the adjacent day care. Living just a few blocks away made it an easy walk to work. Chuck had a full-time job working for the railway, with good pay and regular hours. He attended class in the evenings, and other than the "blip" of infidelity, I thought we had the perfect life. Denial was becoming my best friend.

I had had a miscarriage in the second year of our time in Vancouver, but a few months later I was pregnant again. Soon I delivered the most gorgeous baby girl ever! I remember sitting on the couch with tears of joy running down my cheeks, gazing into my daughter's face as she looked up at me. Ava was perfect. She had beautiful strawberry blond curls. Her jubilant laughter filled our home. Garnet, my rambunctious three-year-old, was delighted with this new addition—so much so that I had to keep my eyes on him as he'd often crawl into her crib "just to hug her." I was the most contented I had ever been. What a joy to be a mom to these beautiful children.

When Ava, my little china doll, was seven months old, my parents came to visit. It was lunchtime after church. I put her in the high chair wearing the lovely pink dress that my mom had bought her. She was sitting very quietly. Dad sat in a chair beside her. When she babbled, Dad jumped. He literally thought she was a doll that I'd dropped into the chair. What a laugh. Dad really loved Ava, and she reciprocated with hugs and kisses. She was a true delight and made our hearts sing.

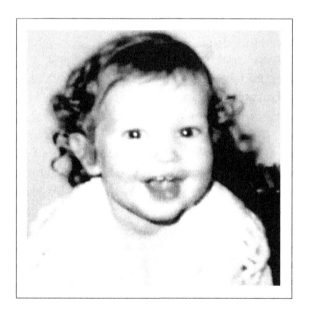

It wasn't long before we were hopping on the city bus for our weekly adventures at Stanley Park. These were delightful times, just me and the kids. Garnet and I would walk, run, explore, and play while Ava watched from her stroller, giggling. As Ava grew, the two of them were inseparable. Their favourite place to go to was the aquarium, especially the "hands on" exhibits. The minute we arrived, Garnet sought out the sea cucumbers, to touch them. He would have stayed at that exhibit for the entire visit. I believe these expeditions to the aquarium led to his lifelong passion with marine life and biology.

Laughter and the joy of small children filled my days until I returned to work when Ava was just six months old. No sooner had I returned to work than I discovered that I was pregnant again. I couldn't help but think of what Chuck had told me years earlier about the doctor's diagnosis that he might not be able to have children. He didn't seem to have any problems whatsoever. We had no issues conceiving.

I had not considered having another child. I thought that we had the perfect family, so this pregnancy caught me a bit off guard. Nevertheless, I quickly embraced it with as much joy as I had the others. This pregnancy, though, was more difficult for me physically.

I was four months along when one Friday evening in May Chuck did not come home from work. It was the May 24 long weekend. I didn't have a vehicle so had no way to get to his place of work. I didn't know the name or have the number of his foreman, so I couldn't call. By late evening, I was distraught.

I called the hospitals in the area, but he was nowhere to be found. I called our pastor and the Bible college. No one had seen him. I hesitated about calling the police. I knew they wouldn't go looking for him right away, and in the back of my mind I really didn't want to know where he might be. He was gone for the entire long weekend.

I felt like I was walking in a fog all weekend. I was sitting on the couch with the kids when he walked through the door on Monday afternoon. He came over and draped his arms around my neck from behind. He smelled of alcohol. My stomach turned and I felt totally repulsed. We didn't drink in our home, and I had never seen Chuck drink since he'd started attending church, let alone come home drunk or with a hangover.

When I told him he stank, he simply said some gay guy had poured wine all over him. Oh, yeah. Good to know. Then, of course, he spilled the beans. He'd gone to a gay bar and spent the weekend with several men. I felt nausea grip me as he started to graphically describe his time with these gay guys. I shut his dialog down quickly—I had no desire to know what they were doing.

Even though he saw how distraught I was, he seemed to get a perverse sense of enjoyment from my reactions. But when he saw the blank look on my face, he began to cry and beg my forgiveness. I recognize now what an incredible actor he was, but at the time I believed that his display of contrition was genuine. What naiveté and gullibility on my part. This very night, after having put the kids to bed, he wanted to make love. How stupid was I? He acted like nothing had happened and that I had no reason to refuse him. I was disgusted. But when I got out of bed, he got angry, got up, and punched me in the stomach. Until now, I'd never refused him. All I could think of as I doubled over in pain was *Has he injured my baby? Will I miscarry?* But after a few days, everything seemed to be normal. I thought I'd better not refuse him again.

The next day Chuck claimed that his behaviour and sexual infidelity were my fault. Well, of course they were. I should have known that. If I would only treat him better. If I would bake more and take better care of him, he wouldn't have to go out looking for sex. *Really?* I had already treated him like the king he thought he was, particularly with his sex-on-demand routine. Although part of me wanted to walk out the door, I had to think of the consequences. I was pregnant and had two other children to think of. So I calmed my fears and caved in, yet again. I prayed ever more fervently for my baby.

In order to better cater to Chuck's will, I started a new morning routine: up at five thirty to bake squares and cookies before making his lunch and serving him breakfast, then rousing the children after he left for work. I continued with this routine for years, somehow thinking that if I could just do better, be better, he would be happy with me.

Time came for the birth of our third child. Having experienced two deliveries, I thought I knew the process fairly well. I had heard many times from other moms that usually labour times were reduced with each delivery. I had delivered Garnet and Ava without drugs of any kind and hoped to do the same again this time. But that was not to be. This delivery was different. This was a posterior birth, and the pain was far more intense. Unlike today, C-sections back then were rare, so the staff attempted to help mitigate the pain with oxygen. It didn't seem to help much. I remember telling the doctor during one long contraction, "This baby is going to kill me."

Nevertheless, after twenty-four hours of labour—ten of those in hard labour—nature had its way and Daniel was finally born in the early afternoon weighing in at ten pounds and measuring twenty-three and three-quarter inches long. I didn't get to see him initially, as he was whisked away immediately to be suctioned. He suffered from aspirating meconium—fecal matter entering the lungs.

Meconium aspiration can occur when a baby takes his first breaths, especially in a difficult delivery, such as Daniel had experienced. He suffered from intense fetal distress during delivery. As he gasped for air, fecal matter entered his lungs. As a consequence,

Daniel quickly became jaundiced. He was a very sick boy for the first few days. For me, though, staying in hospital was a blessing. I was able to get more one-on-one time with my new baby, and it also gave my broken tailbone time to heal. While giving birth is often a difficult process, for most moms the discomfort, pain, and effort is worth it. Gazing into the eyes of a new baby makes all well. Daniel was absolutely gorgeous, and until he got hungry, a very placid child.

Ten days after Daniel's birth, I arrived home still in pain—a lot of pain. But, pain or no pain, my ravenous boy demanded to be fed every two hours. Chuck, being the selfish person he was, let it be known that he was being sexually deprived. We'd never gone that long without having sex, and he wasn't about to let the fact that I was in pain interfere with his voracious sexual desires. He wanted sex, period!

I felt defeated. All I wanted was to get some much-needed sleep, but it was not to be. Chuck didn't much care or give attention to the doctor's advice to abstain from sex for six weeks after a birth. Never had he been concerned about my health or condition after previous births. Why should this one be any different? The difference for me this time was that I had a broken tailbone from the difficult delivery. But the pain that I might suffer seemed inconsequential to him. He wanted his sexual gratification, come what may. As long as he got what he wanted, the pain that others might suffer, no matter who they were, was irrelevant, trivial, and unimportant. This really hit home, later in life, when I found out from my children what they had suffered at his hands during their younger years—palpable evil.

After coming home from the hospital I wondered whether Chuck, given his proclivity to selfishly satisfy his sexual perversions, had sought out sex in my absence. This was the first time that I'd allowed myself to truly consider his infidelity. I didn't like what my mind was telling my heart. I knew the truth, but...

The next few months were exhausting as my tailbone was healing. Chuck did not allow me to have my baby in our bedroom, and the pain I felt contorting my body to feed my new baby was excruciating. When it came time to nurse him during the night, I had to, as gently as possible, slip out of bed, crawl on the floor to the baby's crib in the room across the hall, and then, in order to stand, lift myself up holding on to the bars of the crib. Once standing, I was in less pain. It was the process of standing upright that was most painful.

Finding rest during the day was also difficult, what with a rambunctious five-year-old and two-year-old vying for my attention. But I loved those years with my little ones. When summer came to Vancouver, we went for long walks and played in the park. On rainy days we had to play indoors, of course, but we made the best

of it, playing games of hide and seek, tent building, and building with blocks. How I wish I had had a cell phone in those days. Today I'd have some of the best pictures imaginable, encapsulating some of my favorite memories.

I still laugh remembering the time when my two sisters-in-law, Rachel and Ruth, came to visit us in Burnaby, B.C., a year after Daniel was born. To appreciate the humour here, it has to be explained that almost every street in Burnaby is built on a hill. We were taking all three children to a local park, which meant that we had to walk down quite a steep hill.

Ava and I were walking ahead of the others. Garnet was chatting with Rachel and Ruth while Ruth pushed Daniel down the hill in a collapsible stroller. All of a sudden I heard a scream. I turned quickly, and there was my one-and-a-half-year-old baby careening down the hill toward Ava and me. To give Daniel a little thrill ride, Ruth had decided that she could let go of the stroller for a second or two, let it speed up, and then grab it again. Only the hill was so steep that by the time Ruth tried to regain control of the stroller, it was out of reach. And so the race was on. What a sight—Ruth running full tilt after the stroller, leaving Garnet and her sister far behind. It wasn't so funny at the time, but looking back, and in light of the fact that no one was hurt, it really was pretty funny. I can't help but think that this incident was a harbinger of things to come, when it came to my boys. They are risk takers.

Another incident that same summer was far more serious. The boys were playing outside while I was preparing lunch. I heard someone cry but couldn't see who it was or what had happened. I opened the door and there was Garnet with his arm hanging limply beside him. I called a cab, gathered everyone into the vehicle, and headed for the hospital. Sure enough, he had broken his arm. Unbeknownst to me, a couple weeks previous to this incident his father apparently had held his hand while he walked on the top of the deck railing. That was easy, he thought. Remembering how much fun it had been, this time he thought he'd try it on his own. Well, you can guess what happened. Garnet slipped off the railing and fell fourteen feet, hitting his arm on a rock. It was a miracle that he didn't hit his head.

I learned early on that unless there was serious injury involved, I needed to just go with the flow when it came to my boys. I could set rules, but these boys were risk takers. If there was some kind of conquest to be had, they were all in, dragging their sister along for the ride. Later that year, while climbing onto the top bunk, through no fault of her own Ava slipped on the ladder and fell to the floor, with one of the hooks on the ladder almost taking off the end of her finger. I grabbed her, wrapped her nearly severed finger, and rushed to the hospital. Thank God for our doctors and nurses! They were able to stitch the tip back on. This little lady is now a nurse.

12

North to Alaska (well, not quite)

We spent six years in Vancouver while Chuck completed Bible college. In 1982 we moved our family to Prince George, British Columbia, to help found a church. When we arrived in June, finding housing was virtually impossible, so we ended up pitching our family-sized tent in a campground. Little did I know we would be living there until mid-October.

Many are the times when the things we experience in childhood help us to deal with whatever is thrown at us later in life. This was definitely one of those times. I had grown up roughing it with no running water and an outhouse, so I expect adapting was easier for me than it would have been for most women of my era. What I had experienced during much of my formative years, my children were now experiencing. During the summer, it was a great experience, but as winter approached, not so much.

Chuck had found a day job, and while he was at work the kids and I had fun hiking, swimming, playing, and cooking. Summer is a beautiful time of year in northern British Columbia, with quiet and peace all round. A time and place for reflection. I loved the area and soon began to make friends. There were lots of moms with tots at the campground.

Summer is great, but by early September, fog and rain move in and temperatures begin to drop. The rain and cold made living in a tent with three children seven, four, and two a whole lot more difficult. But, while it often felt like we were living in a three-ring circus, I somehow managed to survive and maintain my sanity and sense of humour. I was thankful that the darkness fell earlier. The kids went to sleep as night fell, and I got some much-needed rest.

Often by October there is snow on the ground and the temperatures drop to below freezing in this area. No problem keeping food from spoiling, but the water was most often frozen come morning. With the onset of winter, we would soon have to move from the park and find more fitting accommodations. When the Thanksgiving holiday rolled around, the park would close. I got very good at keeping a campfire going, boiling water, cooking on a camp stove, and maintaining the basic necessities.

It was almost Thanksgiving when Chuck finally found us a place to rent. Looking back now, I have to wonder why it took so long. Running water and heat never felt so good. After the kids were fed, bathed, and tucked in for the night, I enjoyed the absolute luxury of sinking into a tub filled with steaming water and fragrant bubbles, and reading in peace. Yep, you never miss the water till the well runs dry! To this day, relaxing in a tub continues to be a joy.

The church slowly began to grow in this wonderful community, but as I had young children, my involvement was limited. It came as a surprise to me when I got a call one day from a Native woman from Prince George, 370 kilometres away, asking me for help. She wanted to know whether she could bring her daughter for me to pray over her.

Although I was immersed in the Bible and in personal prayer, praying for and over others was something new to me…but how could I say no? I agreed, and a few days later she and her seventeen-year-old daughter came to our home. Chuck was at work, so thankfully a neighbour agreed to watch the children for a couple of hours.

The mom, in desperation, conveyed her concern for her daughter's health and welfare, as she had started to experiment with drugs. She was concerned that she might be struggling with addiction. I knew absolutely nothing about addictions, and although praying over someone was intimidating for me, I did what seemed natural in the moment and began to pray. Looking back, I see that this was God's hand moving me.

This beautiful young seventeen-year-old was herself desperate, and so I sat on the floor with her and asked God to show me how to pray for her. What I experienced next was miraculous, frightening, yet intriguing. I had a vision that was like watching an old film reel, but in colour. I wish I could say that the scene was pleasant and encouraging, but to the contrary, it scared me.

> *I saw a young girl, perhaps five or so, contentedly digging a hole in the sand on a beach with her little shovel. No one else was in sight. Suddenly she looked out over the water at another little girl, twenty to thirty feet from shore, who was in trouble. Unable to find the bottom, she began to sink. I was panicked. Suddenly the scene went black and everything stopped.*

With tears streaming down my face and my heart palpitating, I had to take deep breaths to regain my composure. I sat quietly for a few moments and asked God to help me make sense of this. The mom and daughter had quizzical looks on their faces, so I told them about the vision.

The daughter immediately slipped to the floor in front of me and held on to me with tears pouring down her face. Between sobs, her mom told me what had happened. She explained that the little girl on the beach, in my vision, was her daughter, the teen before me. What I had seen was what actually had happened to this teen and her older sister. Mom had been distracted preparing a picnic lunch, and her other daughter had ventured out into deep water. Mom had tried to reach her, but it was too late and she was unable to get to her daughter in time. Her eldest child drowned that day.

I was shaken, as were mom and daughter. We hugged one another, crying together. I have little recollection of what else I prayed for over the next couple of hours, but God revealed to me clearly the cause of this teen's grief and her subsequent surrender to drugs. Her grief and pain, along with the insecurities confronting so many teens, became an unbearable load. Her surrender of her deep emotional pain to Jesus helped her turn a new leaf in her life and proved to her that Jesus was real and cared for her.

Although I had heard of people having dreams and visions, I had never experienced such a thing. Was God speaking to me? I am cautious when I tell people about God speaking to me, and while I believe with all my heart that God speaks to people in dreams and visions, I recognize that there have been many who have misused this phenomenon for personal gain. I am careful. Not every dream or vision is of God, but some may be. I continually pray for wisdom and discernment, for His leading and guiding.

The message to me was unequivocal. God had shown me something about His healing power and His desire to restore those in need. I began to delve more deeply into the Bible and discovered that there are many accounts of God's intervention in people's lives through dreams and visions. And, as has been reported more recently, through dreams and visions Jesus is revealing Himself to

Muslims and others around the world even today, bringing many to Himself. I am comforted with the thought that God, by His grace, wanted to use me. While I felt that I was in good company, the question was *How*?

13

A Change of Atmosphere

Peace in our marriage never lasted long. Shortly after this experience, the atmosphere in our home soured. It wasn't that we argued a lot, as I most often acquiesced to Chuck's will. What really caused a rift in our relationship was his continued infidelity.

Chuck encouraged me to find work, so I took a part-time job as a receptionist at a music shop, working four to nine p.m. He was home from work by three and able to watch the children, which seemed to work perfectly. I should have known this was just the calm before the storm. And what a hurricane it became.

We'd been a year in our new location when Chuck once again came home late one Saturday night. I was waiting up. He got right to the point and told me that he had found a new lover. I will never forget his exact words: "I love him and I love you too. I want you both!"

I was absolutely devastated. It had only been a few days since I had experienced the most "magical" event of my young life—a life-altering vision. How could this now be happening? I couldn't speak. I headed to our bedroom and grabbed my Bible. I was so hurt, so wounded, so demoralized. My Bible fell open at the following verses.

The Spirit of the Sovereign LORD *is on me,*

because the LORD *has anointed me to proclaim good news to the poor.*

He has sent me to bind up the brokenhearted,

to proclaim freedom for the captives and release from darkness for the prisoners,

to proclaim the year of the LORD'S *favor and the day of vengeance of our God,*

to comfort all who mourn,

and provide for those who grieve in Zion—

to bestow on them a crown of beauty instead of ashes,

the oil of joy instead of mourning, and a garment of praise instead of a spirit of despair.

They will be called oaks of righteousness,

a planting of the LORD *for the display of his splendor.*

They will rebuild the ancient ruins and restore the places long devastated;

they will renew the ruined cities that have been devastated for generations.

ISAIAH 61:1–4

It was like God was speaking directly to me.

> *Are you kidding me, God? Did you just see and hear what is happening in my family? How do you expect me to help others when I can't even help myself? When our family is falling apart, when my husband is continually unfaithful? When he now wants me to accept his latest suggestion and become party to his perversion? There is no way I can do this!*

My heart was broken, my marriage in shambles, and God wanted me to what? Heal the broken-hearted.

> *I don't think you have the right person, God! I seem to remember You saying somewhere that we need to have our own house in order first. Can't you see what's happening? So thanks, but no thanks!*

I didn't understand at that time how the enemy of our souls (Satan) desires to rob us of everything that God has in store for us. With hardships and trials, he tries to pry us away from God's plans. It worked...for many years. Thirteen, to be exact. I slammed my Bible down and slammed the door on God's message. I was in such pain and turmoil that I really don't know how I made it through the next few days.

For the first time, I recognized and admitted Chuck's selfish depravity. I finally "drew a line in the sand." NO! to Chuck's deviant agenda and his hiding behind the church.

I insisted that he talk to the pastor of our new church about his proclivity to this deviant behaviour. Although I was not party to the conversation, I was advised by the pastor to forgive Chuck and stay in the marriage, if possible.

Of course! There were children to think about, and I took my marriage vows seriously. I did not want to divorce him, but something changed in my heart that day. I tried my best and gave it my all, but I knew I could no longer trust him. I may have closed my Bible, but that scripture would not leave me. Thankfully, God persisted. That scripture has remained with me through the years.

Chuck's abhorrent behaviour continued. A few weeks later, I came home from work emotionally distraught. It was my responsibility to lock up shop at the end of the day. On this particular night, one of the musicians attempted to assault me. I ran out as quickly as I could. When I told Chuck about the incident, his comment was "It would be good for you to have an affair."

There I was again. No protection. No safety. No security. No concern from Chuck. No love or care for me—only what he thought might benefit him. A righteous anger at his immorality grew within me.

14

Back in Ontario

We stayed in Prince George for another year before deciding to move back to Ontario. This is one move that I actually initiated. By this time, we'd moved fourteen times in our ten-year marriage, thankfully only twice interprovincially. I wanted to be closer to family and have my children grow up knowing their grandparents. Chuck, it seems, was wearing out his welcome in northern B.C. and appeared happy with the move.

The move was made back to my hometown. We had no friends, and the reasons for not reconnecting with former high school friends were twofold. Many had moved away, and I was reluctant to make new friends as I was guarded about Chuck's history.

Within a year and after a decade of marriage, at my behest, we purchased our first house. Chuck reluctantly agreed. It turned out to be a great decision even though Chuck wasn't necessarily on board. Housing prices were very inexpensive at the time and our mortgage was manageable. At the moment, we were both employed. We found a church in a neighbouring town about a half hour away. We happily attended whenever possible.

Not long after buying our home, Chuck lost his job and so decided to try his hand at business. Landscaping was what he seemed to enjoy. Although he was decent at it, he had no business sense, and it soon fizzled out, leaving him once again unemployed. Except for the occasional seasonal job of picking apples, Chuck never did go back to work during the rest of our marriage.

I, on the other hand, was now working two different jobs to pay the bills. It was difficult because I was away from the children so much, but, I thought, at least their father was home for them. I loved spending time with the kids at the park or going to the local pool, but the best was being back near the bay and riding our bikes to the local campground to swim.

To some of our neighbours, Chuck seemed like the ideal husband. He cooked the meals and cleaned the house, while I worked outside the home. He'd walk the kids to school, play games in the back yard, and always seemed attentive with them. We were considered a "progressive" family—Mom works, Dad takes care of the home. But "Chuck's other side" was never seen outside the front door.

He was a harsh disciplinarian. In fact, while we'd been living in Vancouver, the Children's Aid Society had been called by a pre-school after our two-year-old daughter arrived with bruises. Chuck had gotten a little too handy with the belt he kept around for discipline. I was thrilled when he was reprimanded by the authorities and told never to use a belt or anything similar again. He actually listened, or so I thought.

15

The End in Sight

In 1987, Chuck once again felt that he needed to clear his conscience. Perhaps it was his involvement in church that helped him maintain a sense of responsibility. Or maybe he just wanted to shock me. Whatever it was, he decided this time to spill it all.

He told me that he had had over twenty-six homosexual affairs, not to mention the orgies, during the thirteen years of our marriage. He was done with it, though, he said. "If I ever do it again, I'll kill myself," he proclaimed. Chuck sounded repentant and sincere, but after all these years, I was slow to buy in. He'd trampled my heart too much. It would be a time of wait, watch, and see. I didn't have to wait long before he once again rocked the entire family to the core.

I came home from work to find the kids playing alone in the living room. Their dad was upstairs, apparently napping. I went up to find him sprawled on the bed, unconscious, with an empty bottle of pain pills beside him. I called 911, turned, and saw my precious little girl, only nine at the time, in the doorway.

The look on her face as paramedics removed her dad from the house was heart-wrenching. She begged to come to the hospital with me, but not knowing whether he would live or die, I thought it best that all three children remain at home. I asked her older brother to watch over his siblings. Was it the right decision? Even in hindsight, it's difficult to know.

I rushed to the hospital. No one knew when he had taken the pills or how long he'd been unconscious. Chuck's attending nurse was an acquaintance of mine. She offered me comfort and solace as she explained the procedure underway. The doctors and nurses immediately pumped his stomach, and then gave him activated charcoal to absorb the chemicals in order to mitigate the toxicity of the overdose. It was now wait and see. What would I have to tell my family?

It wasn't long before Chuck began to respond. The kids' dad was going to be okay. But he was being transferred to another hospital for psychiatric assessment and treatment. Although I was in a daze driving home, I was relieved that I would be able to report to the family that their dad would be all right.

It wasn't until much later that I discovered that the guilt he carried was far deeper than I knew. I was unaware of the extent of the perversions that prompted his suicide attempt.

The depths to which he had stooped would ultimately be revealed, but not before more horrors would be perpetrated.

16

Just a few days after Chuck's suicide attempt, I was simply stepping off the curb on my way to work when I felt a sudden jar in my back. The pain was excruciating, making it difficult to walk. I managed to get a ride to the doctor's office, where I was diagnosed with acute sciatica. It felt like a fire, burning fire down my back and legs. I had to use a cane in order to walk, and even then I was hunched over for nearly six months. I was not one to take medication, but pain meds were all that kept me mobile for those months. I could not afford to miss work, though—I had a family to feed and I had no disability insurance. But my discomfort, pain, and stress didn't seem to matter. Chuck was in his own little world.

Chuck had spent over a month in hospital, resting and getting care. One afternoon as I shuffled into his room, I met his psychiatrist. This lovely man took one look at me and said it was I who needed to be in hospital. He will never know how much those words meant to me. Someone finally validated my pain. Silly as this may sound, it meant the world to me at that moment.

The following week Chuck was released and, as usual, got lots of attention from his mom. Because of his past violent tendencies and the fear that he might again attempt suicide, the children and I felt as though we had to walk on eggshells. Family members claimed that Chuck's attempt to take his life was my fault. They had no idea what had transpired in our home over the years. I felt alone and abandoned.

Now that he was home and I had time to process things, I realized how deeply hurt I felt, like he had taken a knife to my heart. I wanted to feel sorry for him, but I no longer had any empathy for him. His excuses fell on deaf ears.

I had little time, though, to spend wallowing in self-pity. I had three very traumatized and needy children to care for, as well as a husband who was unable to care about much that was happening in our home. It wasn't until two years later, as I was grieving the loss of our marriage, that I began to allow myself to feel the deep pain of rejection he had inflicted. It felt like I had been nothing more than a toy to him to play with sexually and then abandon for his expanding sexual perversions.

17

The Final Straw

I was now working at three different places of employment, just trying to keep our heads above water, while Chuck had not held a steady job in five years. I was doing the very best I could for my family, but little did I know what had been happening at home.

The year after the attempted suicide, I arrived home from work early one afternoon and found Chuck beating our eldest son. He was holding Garnet, now thirteen, up against the wall in the living room and banging him against it. Although I'd witnessed Chuck spanking our children on occasion, I had never seen this kind of behaviour from him before.

To my knowledge he had never used a belt or excessive force since the CAS incident in Vancouver, but here he was abusing our son. Chuck wasn't happy that he'd been caught, but I'd seen more than enough. I ordered him to pack his bags, leave, and never come back. He never lived in our home again. It was the best decision of my life, but this was just the beginning of what I was to learn from our children about Chuck's behaviour.

While it was difficult telling the children that their father would not be coming home, a dark and heavy cloud was lifted from our home that day. I felt a burden being lifted from my shoulders.

And my health, which had been poor and getting worse, began to improve.

One night, not long after Chuck left, I awoke with an overwhelming sense of trepidation. Someone was in my bedroom. In the dark of night, I could feel the presence of evil. I was flooded with fear and looked to see a hand gently pushing my head down on the pillow. Immediately I knew it was an angel of the Lord. He spoke quietly, saying, "Do not look." I continued to pray, now realizing that the "thing" at the end of my bed was not a person who had broken into my house, but rather an evil spirit. For years I thought it was Satan himself. It was a spirit of perversion, so dense it felt I'd been immersed in a black fog. I reached my hand under my pillow. I had taken to keeping my Bible there. As I touched it, peace enveloped my soul and the heavy weight of evil left the room.

I had never confronted the presence of evil like I did that night, although I have had a few lesser experiences since that time. I knew that this evil spirit had something to do with Chuck's depraved behaviour. He had defiled our marriage. Far worse than this was the deplorable abuse he had subjected our children to. I finally became aware of this nearly three years later.

At this point, though, I believed the four of us could put our lives back together and have a sense of normalcy. I had so much yet to learn.

Although my kids seemed bright enough, they struggled in school. Tests showed that two suffered with attention deficit hyperactivity disorder (ADHD) while my youngest suffered with attention deficit disorder (ADD). Unfortunately, in the early eighties there wasn't the kind of help available for kids suffering from these disorders that there is today.

Thankfully, the divorce was finalized in record time. I had no intention of staying in the marriage any longer than necessary. I didn't ask for child support as I figured that it would never happen anyway. At my request, I was given ownership of the matrimonial home. This provision was granted to me by the judge provided that I accept some child support. I asked for a small monthly amount. I received one payment of two hundred dollars but then absolutely nothing for the remaining ten years. This was not unexpected.

I was on my own with the children. Difficult as it was, due to my work schedule I loved it. Emotionally it was far easier now that Chuck was out of the picture. The kids and I spent our time together after school and work as much as we could, although by this time I had teenagers in the house who liked doing their "own thing."

I fondly remember one long weekend in May the year after Chuck left. Because we all loved camping, we decided to head up to Tobermory, a beautiful harbour on Georgian Bay. Thirty years ago there were few RVs and some pop-up campers. Most camped in tents as we did.

We got the tent up and went hiking the first evening, but by the next morning the rain had started. It continued all day. I had brought board games, but after a few hours any novelty was wearing thin. I had a fourteen-year-old, an eleven-year-old, and a nine-year-old to keep separated, along with Ava's kitten she had insisted on bringing along. Roughhousing was one of the boys' favourite pastimes, and the tent was most definitely not the place for it.

When Garnet asked if he could borrow a pillowcase and go exploring in the rain, I thought, *Sure, what could it hurt. I can always replace a pillowcase.* Ava and Daniel joined him. They were gone for several hours. I enjoyed the peaceful sound of the soft rain on the tent and spent the afternoon on my own reading.

I was beginning to think I should head out looking for them when they returned. Garnet was carrying the pillowcase. It was heaving and twisting, obviously filled with something living.

You need to understand something at this point. My children were always bringing home things that crawled or fur babies of one sort or another, all of which they wanted to keep. They were all animal lovers and loved the thrill of capturing hurt or wild creatures. So I was not overly alarmed by the squirming pillowcase—more curious than anything. As they approached, I could see Garnet was struggling a bit to keep a secure hold of the top of the pillowcase. The three of them looked like a pack of wet dogs, Daniel and Ava not nearly as happy and excited as Garnet.

In this pillowcase was a squirming mess of snakes! Yep, you got it. Just about one of every kind they have on the peninsula. Thankfully Garnet did not bring back any rattlesnakes; it's the only poisonous one we have in Ontario. Garnet had already left a green snake and a rare hognose snake with the local park warden, but there were 40 forty snakes left in that pillowcase, including a big mother water snake and her eight babies!

After Garnet had taken each snake out and released it, there in the bottom of the pillowcase was a six-inch fish the water snake had regurgitated. Sorry about the queasy stomach—raising boys is fun, right? Daniel was just about spitting nails as Garnet excitedly talked about catching the big water snake, and when Garnet finished his biology lesson, Daniel enlightened me on how Garnet sent him out on a log to catch the noncompliant babies.

While Garnet had become something of an expert snake catcher over the years, Daniel was a little less enthusiastic. If you know anything about snakes, you know that baby ones can be quite aggressive. These baby water snakes had proved difficult to catch.

Nevertheless Garnet was adamant that Daniel get them because he, Garnet, had to hold the pillowcase. I don't remember the kids getting bitten, but it was early spring and the ice was just off the water and, in the pouring rain, it was a less than thrilling experience for Daniel. I'm not sure if Ava caught any that time or not, but she was usually not to be outdone by the boys.

Needless to say, that pillowcase quickly made it to the dumpster. Some twenty-five years later, while at a wedding, we happened to meet the man who had been park warden that weekend. When asked if he remembered a teenager coming to the office with a pillowcase full of snakes, he laughed and laughed. Said that was the most determined kid he'd ever met. We quickly dialed Garnet's cell and handed it to the former warden.

While life was not always rosy being a single mom, at least there was a sense of calm in our home. Now it was just me and the kids.

Don't say there is no escape

And your troubles wear you out.

The darker the night, the brighter the stars.

The deeper the sorrow, the closer to God.

UNTITLED POEM
APOLLON MAYKOV, 1878

18

A New Chapter Begins

Several months after my divorce, I made a list of the qualities I would look for in a man, should I ever remarry.

- Honesty
- Faithfulness
- Integrity
- Good with children
- A farmer
- A Christian

It may seem odd that I put "Christian" at the end of the list, but I had had a wolf in sheep's clothing once and I wasn't about to be fooled and manipulated again. All of these qualities had to be in place before I would ever again enter into a long-term relationship.

Two years later I met my future husband. It was my friend Bev's fortieth birthday, and to celebrate we went to a single parents' dance. The place was packed and we were sitting at the only table that had a couple extra chairs, when a group of four guys walked in.

Bob, my future husband, asked if he could sit with us, but Bev piped in, "Only if you dance," and dance we did—all night long.

The next time we met, Bob asked if I had two or three children; then he told me that I had seemed familiar to him, but he hadn't been sure why, so after the dance he'd stayed up late into the night trying to figure out where he knew me from. I found out that he had spent the entire night looking through some old local newspapers—a paper I'd sold advertising for—and he'd found my picture.

Was Bob a stalker? His explanation of finding who I was set me on edge. I was reluctant to go out with Bob on my own, so we double-dated, Bob and I and Bev and her new boyfriend. I felt like I was seventeen again—certainly a heady experience. This man seemed genuinely interested in me as a person. Wow! I had never met anyone like him before. Nonetheless, I was cautious. I set boundaries. If the children and I had plans, I wasn't about to change them for any man. I'd learned my lesson well.

One Friday night Bob called to see if I would go for a drive and to the movies the next day. As the kids and I had planned a bike ride on Saturday, I declined. But Saturday morning he called and asked to join us on our bike ride. The children knew that I had been casually dating someone. Perhaps now was a good time for them to meet him. We talked it over and decided that he could join us. It was an hour's drive to our place for Bob.

We could barely suppress our laughter when we saw his bike. Turns out he'd dragged the bike that he had had as a teen out of the barn and spent Friday night fixing it to make it rideable—barely! We really weren't sure that that rusty old thing would make the grade, but it held up just fine. It wasn't until years later that he actually purchased a new bike. I looked at this man in a different light. Here was someone who didn't care about pretty or new. He cared about people. He cared about being with us. He even started coming to church with us.

Bob had two young children from his first marriage, a boy two and a girl three, and he was in the throes of a messy divorce. To his dis-appointment, it dragged on for over a year and a half. We couldn't marry until it was settled, and although we didn't want to compli-cate matters any more than they already were, after several months of dating we decided that it was time for all the kids to meet. With my three kids—two teens and an eleven-year-old—and Bob's two toddlers, we would become a blended family. We would have our respective challenges. Bob had never dealt with teens, and I had to again deal with two kids under five. Considerable adjustments would be in order.

While Bob's divorce saga was unfolding, we had time to get to know each other more intimately. We talked about a great many things, including God, religion, and relationships. Bob had been raised in the United Church and I, a Pentecostal, was jokingly called a Charismanic! Church for Bob went from sedate to live-ly—something he was willing to accept. Bob drove an hour to at-tend Sunday church with us, but never complained. Being a farm-er, he'd do his chores earlier in the morning and then head out to meet us for church. After church, he'd take the kids and me out for lunch and then head home. Sometimes my kids and I cooked lunch at his house.

I remember one night, after a date, sitting in the car telling him what I was looking for in a husband. I wanted a man who was willing to lay down his life for me. Poor guy. It was like taking a sledgehammer and hitting him between the eyes. Subtlety is not one of my strengths, but to his credit, he didn't flinch. Instead, our relationship deepened. We shared our hopes and dreams with each other, the joys as well as the day-to-day struggles. And, since we lived an hour apart, we spent a couple of hours on the phone each night, after the kids had gone to bed.

As our love grew, so did sexual temptations. Bob was a gentleman, and he respected my beliefs regarding sex before marriage, but we were both drawn to one another physically, and at thirty-six, I found myself unwed and pregnant. By this time Bob had been separated from his wife for about two years, but due to custody issues was not yet divorced. Another lesson learned. Step away from God's plan and there are consequences. Our son would be four months old before we could marry.

When I realized that I was pregnant, a decision had to be made. Either Bob was in this for the long haul or he would have to be out of my life immediately. I could not further compromise my life or the lives of our children. I gave Bob time to consider my demands, but to my joy, a few days later he announced that we should marry as soon as possible. Unfortunately, Bob's soon-to-be-ex-wife was in no hurry to sign divorce papers, as she was quite content with the live-in arrangement with her boyfriend.

As my pregnancy developed and with summer coming, Bob and I decided to move my small travel trailer to the farm so that we could all be together. We added beds to the kids' rooms and they settled in the house nicely. I stayed in the trailer.

This arrangement worked fine until I came home from work one day to find that the trailer had been sold! We laugh about it now, but it didn't seem funny at the time. Bob had started selling real estate and perfecting his art of negotiation. Apparently someone needed the trailer more than we did! A new routine began.

Until the birth of our son, I slept at Bob's parents' place, five minutes away. At seven a.m. I'd go to Bob's house to get the kids ready for school and then spend the rest of the day at the farm. At nine p.m., I'd head back to his parents'.

It was around this time that we changed churches. Imagine walking into a church in a small community of approximately one thousand people, where Bob knew most of them, trying to maintain anonymity. Good luck with that. I was apprehensive walking in with our six children, but everyone greeted us with kindness and respect. The love of Jesus amidst this group was incredible. With their encouragement we started to grow spiritually. Four months later, we were married.

19

And Then There Were Eight

Our son of four months celebrated our wedding day with us. While we may have had things backward, Bob and I were committed to raising this family together, and we've never looked back. Our blended family lived in Bob's small house on the family farm. It was just 675 square feet on the main floor with a two-piece bath, and three bedrooms and a bathroom upstairs.

Looking back, I marvel at how we managed to pack six children into two bedrooms, but we did. Three boys slept in one bedroom, two girls in another and the baby in a crib in our room. This wasn't unusual for large families. I was grateful for the age differences. My boys at the time were sixteen and eleven; Bob's son was four. My daughter was twelve and Bob's daughter five. The older children enjoyed the younger ones, and Bob's children looked forward to tagging after their new stepsiblings.

We seemed to repeatedly be in a custody battle yearly with Bob's ex-wife. For several years, while the children were young, they lived primarily with us. This was wonderful. They loved their dad and their life on the farm and were thrilled to have siblings—well, most of the time!

Bob's daughter Amy loved tromping around the fields with the big boys almost as much as she liked playing house in the tree fort with Ava. One day they'd been out "tipping round bales." These bales weigh approximately twelve hundred pounds each. Daniel and Garnet liked to tip them up to see what critters might be lurking underneath. They had taken a box out with them to hold any unlikely creatures they found. I was looking out the kitchen window when they returned with Amy squealing with delight as usual. She was picking up mice one by one out of the box and putting them in an old aquarium Garnet had found in the barn. Pretty mellow, so I continued peeling potatoes.

Soon I heard more laughter from the (by then) six-year-old. I opened the back door to see what she was up to. We had a litter of six-week-old kittens, and she was putting the kittens in the aquarium with the mice. I'm not sure which animals were more surprised, the traumatized mice or the curious kittens! No animals were injured in this experiment, and the mice were subsequently released back in the bush, well away from the house. Ahhh...life on the farm.

One afternoon the older boys were haying with Bob. This was a new experience for them. Although Garnet had worked a bit cutting lawns, he really hadn't had to do much physical labour till now. Daniel at eleven was less than impressed, but it was a "necessary evil," so to speak, if we wanted to feed the cows and survive the winter.

They brought the wagon back to the barn and were starting to unload. Amy decided she would, with the help of the guys, climb to the top of the load, which was relatively safe as long as she didn't go near the edge when she got to the top.

Before you gasp, "safe" for farm kids looks a whole lot different than for city kids. Much to my chagrin, walking the high beams of the barn was one of the favourite pastimes of the older kids. To this day none of them have a fear of heights.

But I digress—back to the top of the hay wagon. I heard Amy yelling. Not a fearful scream, but a scream of excitement. I could see her jumping up and down, pulling on something. One of the boys walked over to her and, lo and behold, she was pulling on the tail of a snake that was caught in the bale of hay. The snake was long dead, but that wasn't the point. This little girl, as much as she liked to dress up like her sister, was no Miss Prissy for sure! What a hoot.

In the very early morning one day the next spring, we heard a bleating out in the barn. Cows don't bleat, and we didn't have sheep, so we were perplexed for a couple minutes until we saw a doe standing off to one side of the pasture. Garnet, not taking the time to throw some pants on, ran out to the barn in his underwear and came back to the house holding a newborn fawn. By this time all the children were up, and each got to see this beautiful little creature before Garnet released him across the fence to his waiting mom. We watched as she licked her baby, then sauntered off into the woods.

Another incident involved Garnet and our new pup. My mom had bought him a pair of new high-top red runners. Back then our kids didn't get much in the way of new clothes, so these runners were his pride and joy. And, like in many families, children—and even sometimes the adults—occasionally left their stuff lying around, getting underfoot in the small front hall.

I was in the habit of cleaning up: putting things back where they belonged. In this particular case, I placed Garnet's new runners at the top of the steps. It never occurred to me that the new pup might set claim to them as his own, promptly chewing the top of the runners to shreds. Garnet was so upset, and rightfully so.

Nothing compares to life on the farm. I have thanked God repeatedly for the privilege of living and raising children here. While there was lots of work on the farm that we weren't used to, my older kids loved it there. This was their home. Even though Garnet was sixteen by the time Bob and I married, the farm became his safe place that he called home until he married.

Of course we had our challenges with six children, as would be expected. Our biggest challenge was when Daniel began acting out, but I'll get to that later. Thinking about my children now, and the compassionate adults they've become, fills me with joy and brings a balm to the years of hurt and pain we have all experienced.

20

Our World Falls Apart

Our lives were about to be turned upside down once again. Things in our new blended family had been moving along nicely, and I was at peace. But that peace was about to be shattered. One night after supper, I was busily cutting Daniel's hair when he suddenly blurted out, "Mom, Dad sexually abused me."

What? No parent wants to hear this. I was stunned. *Did I really hear what I thought I heard?* Were my ex-husband's acts of terror and the brutalizing of my kids still with us?

I can't remember what my exact response was at the time, but even now, I can still feel the shock and pain I felt in that moment. I called Bob in from the barn and conveyed to him what I had just heard. Bob, Daniel, and I found a quiet place to talk—not an easy task in such a small house with kids running around.

We sat together on the couch and Daniel began to disclose the story of his abuse. Over time, many more horrors would be revealed. What we found out that night was just the tip of the iceberg. The truth of what my son had endured at the hands of this predator, his biological father, was starting to unfold. For Daniel, the pain of telling the story of his abuses must have been like repeatedly tearing a dressing off a wound. It took a long time and many interviews by the police and Children's Aid before a complete picture of his pain was revealed.

My ex-husband had been out of the picture for some time. He had not visited the children in three years, nor had he paid support. He had immersed himself in a gay life-style. When the police picked him up, he was living with a boyfriend in Montreal.

When Daniel heard that Chuck had been brought to a nearby jail, he became stricken with anxiety. Until then he had never displayed

 obsessive-compulsive behaviour; now he began locking doors and being so fearful. Bob could see the panic in my son and so sat him down to try to find out what was behind this change in him. Daniel said, "I'm afraid my father will come after me and kill me."

I'll never forget Bob's response: "If he ever steps foot on this property, I'll nail his balls to the fence post!"

I'm sure my jaw dropped, but Daniel laughed—in fact, we've laughed at that comment since. While Bob had never even been in a childhood fight, we knew that he would do whatever it took to protect his family.

We reassured Daniel that we would take care of him, and at his request we started locking our doors at night. We encouraged him to wake us up whenever he had a nightmare or was afraid. He could come to us at any time. That night he gave us each a big hug—something he'd not done in a long time.

Resting in the trust that he had in Bob, his stepdad, Daniel never again checked the door locks. He had found someone he could trust with his life. For me, this spoke volumes about who Bob is. Here was a real man. While Daniel's anxiety and fear of his father and men in general did not leave him, he saw that there was hope.

part two

THE ~~CHILDREN~~

21

Daniel Tells His Story

Today we are on a fishing trip with Daniel. As I revealed in the preceding chapter, he was the first of my children to disclose the horrific physical, sexual, and mental abuse committed against him by the hands of his biological father. Over the years, Daniel disclosed bits and pieces of his sufferings. I kept a journal to record the history of the abuses that he discussed with us. It proved helpful while he was being interviewed by the police and later in court. This chapter chronicles the events.

Daniel, now forty years old, is holding his newest rescued pet—a beaver about six weeks old that loves all the attention he's getting. Although Daniel tops the height chart at 6'8", he has always been known as "the gentle giant." He has a big heart for animals and for suffering children.

Daniel remembers things from the tender age of four. He begins here.

I'd been playing outside with the other kids and decided to go inside for something. As soon as I opened the door, I could tell he [his father] was angry, really angry. He yelled, "What did you do wrong?"

I said, "I don't know." I had no idea what he was talking about. He start-

ed coming for me as he continued to yell. "Tell me what you did wrong!" I remember being really scared. I ran around the table trying to get away from him, and he chased after me. I tried laughing, hoping he'd believe this chase was funny and begin to calm down. The attempt backfired.

Instead, he pushed the table toward me until he had me pinned against the cupboards so hard that my ribs hurt. Then he grabbed a broom and started beating me on the shoulders. Somehow I managed to move the table just enough to drop down and get under it, hoping against hope that he'd stop and walk away.

But it was not to be. He grabbed me by my legs and then threw me headfirst onto the couch. He then removed his belt and began to beat me on the bum, all the time screaming, "Tell me what you did wrong; tell me what I want to hear." I was sobbing so hard I couldn't have answered even if I did know, but he just kept at me. I don't know how long this went on until finally one of the other kids came in, and he stopped.

Immediately after Daniel recounted this horrific event, he stated, "We were lucky, though; we got to play outside a lot." It was amazing how, even as an adult, he chose to immediately switch gears, so to speak, and suppress painful emotions.

I thought about how each of us deals with our emotions outwardly—emotional expressions. Emotional expressions can be seen as a continuum. From extreme minimizers—such as my children, who in order to survive suppress painful thoughts and feelings that surface—to those individuals who are extreme catastrophizers. You may have met a few. These are individuals who see a simple thing like leaving an umbrella at home when it's raining as traumatic.

In my counselling practice, I've found that most complex trauma survivors are prone to minimizing their experiences. Denial becomes a big part of their lives. It helps to keep them sane, or so they hope. Unfortunately, it doesn't help heal the wounds and often, as in the case of my children, causes them to be more easily enticed into an addictive lifestyle, bringing the likelihood of suffering even more abuse.

MINIMIZERS   EMOTIONAL   CATASTROPHIZERS
                             REGULATION

As we continued our talk, I encouraged Daniel to talk about both the good and the bad of childhood memories. Caution: the following contains graphic sexual descriptions.

I remember the yellow banana seat bike I had. I loved that bike, and my father taught me how to ride it. Once I learned to ride, I went everywhere around town. I loved the sense of freedom it gave me, and it got me away from home and what happened there.

We went camping at every opportunity. I loved camping, but he destroyed that for me for a long time. Mom was working, so we'd pack up and head up the river nearby our town and set up camp. On this particular day—I think I was around seven—my brother and sister had gone exploring, but he kept me at camp. Once the other kids were out of sight, he took me into the tent...and raped me.

Our home became a house of horrors for me. It was never safe if Dad was home.

The boys' bedroom was upstairs, the A-frame facing the yard. You could only walk upright in the centre of the room under the peak. Ava's bedroom was at the top of the stairs. We heated with a woodstove. and we had an old wood cooking stove.

The sexual and physical abuse I remember had started when we lived in Vancouver, where I was born and lived until I was two years old. It continued when we moved to Prince George. I was only three when we moved from B.C. back to Ontario, yet I remember many years later the names of two of the men who were friends of my father in Vancouver. These men, invited by my father, had sexually abused me. I was just a toddler.

Dad's brutal abuse escalated when we moved to Ontario. It was his hometown, so he had lots of connections in the area. He began bringing boyfriends into the house when Mom was working and the other kids were at school.

There were three or four guys who regularly visited to have sex with

Chuck, and then they would rape me. Sometimes only one of them, other times all of them, one at a time while the others watched. Other times Chuck or the others would masturbate on me, or they'd have sex with each other and then make me participate.

Chuck would make me watch them all have sex and then force me to comply with their wishes. They fondled me, masturbated on me, and raped me. Chuck was always standing by giving his approval. Afterward, I was given some kind of treat. No matter what, though, when he came looking for me, I would run and hide. He would often whip me with the leather belt for not wanting to participate.

What kind of a father would do that to his son?

22

Shelter in the Storm

Daniel continues his story:

I was a timid child and very shy. I was also terrified of my father. I never told my mom of any of the abuse until after she remarried. Our new family brought me a sense of peace. This was the first time I had ever felt safe around a man other than my grandpa, who loved to take me fishing.

After experiencing true evil, I knew almost immediately that this man, my stepdad, who I now call Dad, was not only kind but respectful of me. He was honest and a genuinely good man. Nonetheless, I didn't make it easy for him. I was a highly traumatized teenager, and I took a lot of my anger out on my new dad as well as myself. I told my stepdad that the anger I felt for my biological father, I took out on him.

Because I (Ann, aka Mom) had kept a journal from the time of my divorce in 1988, I could easily verify Daniel's story and timeline. After Daniel disclosed the events to Children's Aid Services (CAS) and the police, he began having nightmares and terrible

113

headaches. He also became hypervigilant, a frequent symptom of posttraumatic stress disorder (PTSD). He grew extremely anxious and fearful; checking doors and windows to make sure the house was secured. This behaviour worsened when the police told us they were going to pick up Chuck, who was then living in Montreal. Their intent was to bring him back to face child abuse charges.

After Daniel, then eleven, disclosed some of the abuses he had suffered, we wondered whether our other two kids, Ava and Garnet, might have similar horror stories. We sat them down and, without going into details, told them that their father had been arrested for sexual abuse charges against Daniel.

I remember asking whether either of them remembered ever having been sexually abused by their father. At the time, both denied it. Ava was especially adamant in her denial. Soon thereafter, however, Garnet recalled his father giving him a "sex education lesson" at about seven or eight years old. Chuck had masturbated in front of him and encouraged him to do so as well.

When he mentioned this, I remembered the incident. They were in Garnet's bedroom, and I walked in on them in the midst of this "lesson." I immediately challenged Chuck. His words: "Fathers need to teach their sons like this!"

"Not in my house!" I declared. "Don't you ever do that again!"

Of course, in my continued naïveté and imprudent blind trust, I assumed that he would respect my wishes. I lived with the idea that, if or when I was confronted with wrongdoing, I would immediately stop. Foolishly, I believed others did the same. Was I naïve, or did I simply not want to believe what, in my heart, I knew was true? Chuck was a pervert.

I'll share Garnet's story in another chapter. Now back to Daniel.

A few days after Daniel disclosed the abuses; I informed the police and gave my testimony. Daniel was asked to tell his story over five painful and gruelling hours. Afterward, I was given Daniel's statement to read. It tore me apart to think that the man I had called my husband had repeatedly raped my little boy over a six-year period, from ages two to eight. What incredible evil.

I was guilt-ridden. Where had I been? How could I have been so blind? How was it possible that I didn't know what was going on in my home right under my nose? Here was the man whom I had trusted to care for my children while I was at work, and all the while he was abusing them. I had known of his homosexual affairs, but this? In the hopes of keeping my marriage together, I had overlooked Chuck's evil proclivities and in so doing hurt my children.

It took me many years to forgive myself for being so blind. It took years for me to understand that predators such as Chuck are master manipulators who cover their tracks well. By threatening them, he kept the kids from crying out for help. In fact, they were so afraid of him that they never even told each other about their sexual abuse.

Other Victims & Continued Investigation

A few days after Chuck's arraignment, an Ontario Provincial Police constable told us he'd been talking with Chuck's youngest brother, who had also been assaulted by Chuck throughout his childhood. We discovered that a year before Daniel's disclosure, Chuck's sister had told her parents that Chuck had abused her as well. The night of Chuck's arrest, three of his siblings called to convey their appreciation that all this was coming to light. They regretted not having spoken out earlier. Tearfully, they acknowledged that, had they done so, perhaps they could have prevented the abuse of nieces and nephews. It is mind-boggling what hold pedophiles can have on their victims by instilling in them the fear of retribution, should they speak out.

Chuck's family initially wanted him to stay in jail. In late September, bail had been set at $2,500, but no one posted it. His incarceration lasted until mid-October, when one of the sisters called me to say Chuck's dad had posted bail. She was really angry, but we both knew how Chuck could play the victim and wear people down. One doesn't have to look too hard within the LGBTQ community to see how playing the victim has been perfected in order to demand and get special rights. And Chuck had perfected it.

It took two years to get to trial. As the police needed to continue their investigation, they took Daniel to the campsite where he'd been abused. It was painful for Daniel to relive those events. All the while, Daniel was having flashbacks that caused him many sleepless nights.

It was unfortunate, but perhaps understandable, that Chuck's mother, not wanting to face and admit to what her son had done, tried to sweep things under the rug. She insisted that her children stop bringing up the child abuse issues. She didn't want to hear about them. By ignoring his abuses, perhaps she felt she could maintain a sense of peace with Chuck. What she didn't realize was that by sweeping things under the rug, she was inadvertently sacrificing the mental health of her children. As a mom, I understand the deep desire to protect our children, even adult children. But the refusal to face reality can only lead to more pain, especially for the victims.

23

The Verdict

For my children, disclosure of the abuses was just the beginning. The investigation, the trial, and the ensuing and lingering impact of sexual trauma have taken their toll on all of us.

The police told us that this was one of the worst cases of child sexual abuse they had ever encountered. Although there were other victims, the Crown attorney had decided that Daniel's testimony was so solid and accurate that there was no need for others to testify. Back then, twenty-eight years ago, I didn't question their wisdom. I assumed they knew what they were doing. After all, it was their job to represent Daniel. I knew that the truth had been told, and I was confident that this predator would be found guilty.

My son was not at court the day of the verdict. He had asked to go on his grade 8 school trip, and I thought that was just what he needed. He needed to be a kid again. We had just completed four gruelling days in the courtroom with Daniel painfully reliving each moment of the abuses as he testified. The long-overdue case against "The Predator" was finally coming to an end. Today the verdict would be read.

I sat in the courtroom with my husband on one side and Daniel's school psychologist on the other. Chuck sat up front with his lawyer, a little man who gave me the creeps. Reporters were scattered around, but other than that, the courtroom was relatively empty, something for which I was thankful. The judge came in and the process began.

In the early nineties, Daniel was required to testify before the court, with The Predator sitting beside his lawyer at the front of the room. It had been horrendous to sit through the testimony, and I can't even begin to recount the toll it took on my son. He, at thirteen, was incredibly courageous.

The judge talked about my son's courage and his willingness to go through such a difficult process. At the end of the judge's speech, he turned in my direction and stated, "I totally believe your son's testimony, but I can't disbelieve every word his father has spoken. Therefore...he's acquitted."

What had he just said? I will never forget those words. My heart stopped. What? My mind couldn't comprehend the words. Everything seemed to move in slow motion.

NO! NO! NO! There must be some mistake. The judge must have made a mistake. How could he let The Predator off like that? He was going free, while my son would suffer lifelong emotional pain caused by this evil animal? *No, this can't be happening.*

Over at the defendant's table, jubilation, high fives, and smiles all round. I was in such shock that I couldn't cry and simply got up and headed to the door. I came face-to-face with The Predator. He had a dirty, filthy smile on his face. I've never felt such anger and hatred as I felt in that moment. I wanted to punch the brute in the mouth. I approached him screaming how I hated him for the evil he had committed on his family. My husband, the psychologist, and the Crown attorney quickly stepped in and led me from the room. The reprobate was going free.

Ever since then I have wondered why no other witnesses had been called, only Daniel. I also have wondered about the judge's motives. What was his deal? How could he let The Predator go? What other evil lurked in the bushes?

24

Daniel Continues His Story

I was so glad I wasn't at the trial the day the verdict was read. After the verdict, I lost faith in the whole justice system and began to rebel against authority. At fifteen, I began experimenting with drugs: first pot, then coke, and then acid. I also started breaking the law by committing minor crimes: break and enters round our local area.

I had learned early in life how to steal. My first victim was a lady who had befriended me. My brother will share this story in his chapter. Since I was a follower and easily led, I learned from a friend how to steal cigarettes and cash from a small variety store in a little hamlet nearby. I couldn't have been very good at it, as I was soon caught and apprehended.

The police were called, and they sent out their canine unit. My so-called friend and I were on the run. When we heard the dogs, I panicked. Running as fast as I could, I headed through a swamp. The dogs weren't hindered at all by the mud and water, and so they caught me in no time. I was terrified, but I have to say the police were not aggressive, even though they faced this really tall kid. I was tall, but just a kid.

After I was booked, they called my mom to ask that she bring me some dry clothes. She was so angry with me that she asked that I be kept overnight. She had every right to be angry with me. I was sent to a detention centre for six months. Unfortunately, in those six months, I honed my craft of stealing.

After my release, and in order to support my drug habits, I began to steal from my parents, my grandparents, and anyone else I could. I became aggressive at home, even to the point of hitting my sister, whom I loved. I became more and more unruly, and Mom had had enough. She called the police and they took me away. Ava was upset because she was afraid that I would blame her for getting me into trouble. Although I was convicted, my parents went to bat for me and the judge agreed to send me to Teen Challenge, a Christian youth addiction centre, for one year.

This was a great experience, but I almost blew it. By the fourth month, the centre staff had had enough of my belligerence and wanted me out. In the meantime, I had made some good friends – but even though I loved the Bible studies and fellowship, I continued my destructive ways. Once again my parents came to my rescue, and because of their intervention, I was allowed to complete the year.

I hold on to a scripture that has become my life verse. It comes from Jeremiah 29:11-13.

> For I know the plans I have for you, declares the Lord,
>
> plans to prosper you and not to harm you,
>
> plans to give you a hope and a future.
>
> Then you will call on me and I will listen to you.
>
> You will seek me and find me when you seek me with all your heart.

After completing the program, I again moved home. I was now seventeen. Things went well for the first few months, but when I turned eighteen my older brother introduced me to clubbing. It wasn't long before I was doing drugs again, but this time heroin became my friend. Mom and Dad had had enough of my behaviour and so drove me to live with my brother, not realizing that he was facilitating my drug journey.

Not long thereafter, I moved to another city where I reconnected with a Teen Challenge friend who was also struggling. It was here that I met a young woman who was living on the street at the time. We decided to move in together. That lasted all of four months, but after three months, I found out that she was pregnant with my baby, and she was planning to keep it. I was nineteen years old. We were messed up.

I remember going home one weekend to tell my parents about my former girlfriend who was pregnant with my baby. They accepted the news with as much grace as they could muster, knowing that they were going to become grandparents and I was going to be an absentee father.

During the course of the pregnancy, I met a young woman on a blind date. She was beautiful and fun. She was also caught up in the club scene. Nevertheless, we really hit it off, fell in love, and decided to get married. Mom and Dad didn't know about the life we were living, but they liked her and encouraged me to settle down. We married in 2003, but it didn't last. Due to my addictions, we were divorced some time later. However, she has remained a good friend.

25

Daniel's Adult Life

Initially we lived in Kitchener, where I worked driving heavy equipment while my wife completed her teaching degree at the University of Waterloo. I loved my job and our life. My wife loved my infant son, and we attempted to visit him several times a month. Mom was committed to having him one weekend a month, which worked fine for my former girlfriend as it gave her time to party. It was a two and a half hour drive each way for my mom, and in winter the roads were treacherous when it stormed. Mom never missed her weekend.

I had been married for but a short time when I received a Thanksgiving dinner invitation from my biological father. I hadn't seen him in over twelve years. He was back in Toronto, living with a new boyfriend.

I'm not sure what I expected but agreed to visit him in the hopes that he had changed. Sadly, it wasn't to be. He'd cooked Thanksgiving dinner with all the trimmings. I went to the bathroom to wash up and saw a large poster on the wall. It was of a naked teenage Mexican boy, definitely underage. I wanted to throw up. Nothing had changed. He was still lusting after children. I grabbed my things and left. I haven't seen him since.

There were several times that I wanted to kill him or at the very least give him a good beating for what he did to us. The saddest thing is that he walked away from the trial—acquitted! Yet I have no doubt he, like most pedophiles, is still continuing his reign of terror.

I know that the abuse I suffered at his and his buddies' perverse hands sent me down a destructive road, a path where I felt that only with drugs could I help to soothe my emotional pains. Unfortunately, this also caused my family incalculable pain. In the brief time that I was with him, I was again confronted with his evil. He was continuing to flaunt his sexual deviance and getting away with it, hiding openly under the LGBTQ+ umbrella.

My wife and I were both doing drugs and drinking. I had become a functioning addict. As if that wasn't enough, I became a drug dealer. In the midst of this, my wife announced that she was pregnant and immediately dropped the drugs. She asked me to stop too. She wanted a new beginning. She started to attend church and began to change her lifestyle. I resisted. I was not yet ready to go down that path. Drugs were my medication and I thought, No problem, I can have my cake and eat it too!

When my second child was born my first child, Josiah, who had been born to my former girlfriend, was almost five. We purchased a town house in London, Ontario, to be closer to Josiah.

For the next year we tried to live a normal life, yet I was still doing drugs. I tried to stop a couple times. I even entered a drug rehab centre paid for by my employer. I had made some progress when a work accident wiped it all out.

Stepping out of a large backhoe, I miscalculated the distance to the ground and stepped onto the side of a ditch, badly twisting my ankle. I ended up in a walking cast. I was in a lot of pain, and although the doctor was aware of my drug history, he nonetheless prescribed Oxycontin for me. My downward spiral began again. I tried to get off the Oxy cold turkey, but to no avail. I was a mess and spiraling out of control.

A renewed relationship with heroin was on the horizon. I saw it as the way I could cope. As heroin began to consume my life, my wife and I started fighting over my choices. I would work all day and deliver drugs at night. It didn't take long before I was arrested and charged with possession.

What no one knew at the time was that I was stealing from opposing construction companies, stealing from one and selling to the other. This scam lasted several months before I was again arrested, but this time charged with a much more serious crime. Understandably, my wife at this point had had enough and asked me to leave. I was in freefall.

26

When You Think It Can't Get Worse

Drugs, pending convictions, and the loss of my family cast me into a deep state of depression. Although I contemplated suicide, I refused to give up heroin. I felt that it was the only thing that could effectively medicate my emotional pain.

I was convicted of illicit drug use and of theft and sent to the jail in London, Ontario.

After a very short stay, I was to be moved to a minimum-security fa cility in northern Ontario. On the day of the move, I stood in a line with several other guys, awaiting transport. I asked a simple question, but one of the guards flipped out and punched me squarely in the mouth. Seven other guards joined in and repeatedly kicked me in the ribs, stomped on my handcuffed wrists, legs, and feet, and punched me in the head. I was then thrown back into solitary confinement, and although I had been severely beaten and was barely conscious, they refused to take me to hospital.

130 | ANN E. GILLIES, PH.D.

As a result of this beating, I suffered immediate and long-term injuries. I was truly in a bad way. I had a severe concussion and extensive facial lacerations. I lost five teeth and needed reconstructive surgery on my nose and upper jaw. I required several dental implants. My wrist and ankle had been broken, and several of my ribs had been fractured. But the worst of it was that I have since suffered epileptic seizures.

Also as a result of these attacks on my person, an investigation of the entire facility was launched. Eight guards were suspended and four were fired. But for me, I lost what little hope I had left of doing anything with my life. My despair deepened.

Following my release, I rented a basement apartment in our city and in no time got involved with a gang connected to the Hell's Angels. Things went from bad to worse. I delved ever deeper into drugs, which in turn led to more and more criminal activity. Breaking and entering became a way of life. By this time, my drug of choice was crystal meth.

Before too long I was again arrested, but this time I was sent to a maximum-security facility with murderers and rapists. One of the Hell's Angels guys whom I knew was there for pistol-zhipping a retailer. He got fifteen years. My sentence was far shorter, but that prison was a dangerous place to be.

I'd been there for four months before I was allowed to call a lawyer. Standing in line for what seemed like an eternity, I finally got through.

But just as the lawyer answered at the other end of the line, I was attacked by a knife-wielding inmate. Apparently it was his turn to use the phone. I dropped the phone to defend myself. Within minutes guards arrived to separate us. I was thrown into solitary confinement for fighting.

The warden reviewed the tape of the incident and determined that I had only been defending myself. He ordered that I be put into a minimum-security facility. I feared for my safety and asked to remain in solitary. I spent the next three months there until I was moved to a new facility.

Upon my release after having served my sentence, I was given a bus ticket to a city about an hour from my parents. I arrived with just the clothes on my back and moved into a men's home next to the terminal. This environment was rife with addicts, and before too long and for the next two years, things worsened. I became a homeless addict strung out on meth, often suffering bouts of drug-induced paranoia. On more than one occasion my parents went looking for me, only for me to hide from them. I had been convinced that they were part of a sting operation looking to arrest me. Looking back, how difficult it must have been for them, especially my mom. But Mom never gave up on me. To many, including myself, I was a lost cause, but Mom never gave up praying for her lost child.

Half a year later I found myself standing on a bridge overpass ready to end it all. Morning was approaching, and as I watched the drivers go by, a thought screamed at me. How could I do this to someone—jump off into their path? How could I foist such trauma on someone I didn't even know? I stepped back from the brink, took out my phone, and called my parents, asking them to meet me in the city. Always support-ive, they were there in no time.

Only Mom can clearly articulate the events of that day.

It was early Sunday morning. Bob and I were watching a video of a preacher whom I had never heard before. His message was powerful. It was during that message that we received the call from Daniel asking us to pick him up. His voice conveyed panic, and he sounded paranoid. We jumped in the car and headed out.

We found him in the inner city waiting for us. He was in bad shape physically and mentally. It was eight thirty in the morning, so we decided to go to a restaurant for breakfast. I'll never forget Daniel's state. His head hung low as he walked into the restaurant. He looked like a beaten dog, scanning back and forth, on the lookout for cops. In his state of paranoia, he insisted that we sit in a booth near doors and windows. He wanted to know who might be coming into the restaurant.

He wolfed down the food as though he was afraid someone would take it away. Watching and listening to Daniel in his condition was heartbreaking. But, unbeknownst to us and in answer to prayers, God was beginning to intervene in Daniel's life.

We left the restaurant uncertain as to where to take him. As we got into the car, I decided that we should listen to the short ten-minute message given by the pastor we had been watching when Daniel called us. It was about spiritual bondage and the power of God to free us. Daniel started to focus on what was being said. At the end of the message, we cautiously broached the topic, and although wary, Daniel was willing to join our conversation. God was tugging on his heart and showing us what needed to be done.

The long journey of rehabilitation had begun. We were under no illusions. This would be a long and arduous process, but worth it. Daniel moved in with friends who ran an AA/Narcs program. But on many journeys there are bumps in the road, and this road was no different.

27

All Is Not Rosy

In no time at all, Daniel became involved with a woman who asked him to move in with her, which he did. Unfortunately, this girl-friend, herself a druggy, had never gotten clean. But, while it wasn't long before Daniel started using again, something was different. He had a desire to quit. After two years together they sold their house and moved to a remote place in northern Ontario. In hind-sight, this was a Godsend. Daniel was able to camp and fish when-ever he desired. Here, nature offered him peace and tranquility. This was a place like no other, a place to recover. But, as lodging was scarce, they ended up camping on Crown land for months. Good thing it was summer.

Daniel Continues His Story

I was moving toward being drug free, but I wasn't quite there yet.

After moving north, my girlfriend and I decided to quit drugs, and a year later I was able to proudly declare that I had been clean for over a year—the first time since I was a teenager. We began attending a church in town. The pastor was great. He had lots of experience with addicts and was familiar with the local rehab centre. We were soon able to buy a small two-bedroom house that backed onto acres of woodland, complete with a small creek that ran along our property. And it was about twenty minutes from the church. The following winter we were married. But we had issues.

One thing we, as addicts, have difficulty learning is how to do relationships well, and it didn't take long before we were continually arguing. Mom suggested that we both needed counselling, and so I began online sessions with a therapist who specialized in abuse cases. I really liked him and the sessions were good, but things at home were getting worse by the day.

My wife had never given up alcohol. She drank continuously, and the more we argued, the more she drank. When she drank, she became violent. Shortly after we were married, her brother came to visit. They got into an argument, and before long she punched him in the face, breaking his nose. She thought it was funny, exclaiming, "That's how we handle arguments in our family."

After eleven years, I was still embroiled in the lawsuit I had filed against the jail guards who had beaten me. Even though the internal investigation of my beating found that I suffered undue harm at the hands of the guards—many of whom had been dismissed—the Crown asked to have the case dismissed on grounds that I was still an addict. My incarcerations since the beating didn't help my cause.

On the advice of my lawyer I dropped the case, as the legal fees would have eaten up what money I might have been awarded had I won, and there was no guarantee of that. The good news was that I was getting my life turned around, or so I thought.

The arguments with my wife escalated to the point where we had physical altercations. During one such incident, after drinking heavily, she attacked me with an exacto knife, stabbing me twice. I called the police but no charges were laid. After all, I am 6'8" and I have a record. She called the police multiple times after that and finally demanded a divorce. After a year of being clean, I relapsed and had a three day pity party. I was so disappointed in myself.

Once again she called the police—only this time, I was escorted off our property and told not to communicate with her. We had only been married six months, and while I had not been an innocent bystander in our disputes, I was devastated. I was in deep despair. Was there any hope for me? My dreams had been shattered. I felt like I wanted to kill myself.

A friend found me a motel room that my dad paid for, as once again I had no money. Even though I was a six-hour drive away, Mom and Dad visited me a few times and each time took me fishing. We had such fun. I loved watching my mom reel in a fish, yelling and laughing with excitement.

Even though we were under strict orders not to communicate with one another, my wife sent me hundreds of text messages. There were times when I wanted to respond, but to avoid potential problems with police I never again corresponded with her. I needed to get away, and after speaking with Mom and Dad, I'm now living with them. It's not where I wanted to be at forty-one.

I realize that most, if not all, of my sufferings in adulthood have been self-inflicted, and I cannot keep blaming others for the consequences of my poor choices.

I've often wondered how my life might have turned out differently had I not been abused by my pedophile father during the first eight years of my life.

28

Garnet Tells His Story – Chronology of Abuses

What follows are the abuses I suffered – laid out in chronological order and in three parts – that led to a nervous breakdown at the age of forty.

I include here my subsequent and life-changing breakthrough, told from my perspective. Hopefully skipping around on the timeline of how my relevant experiences at different periods in life affected and changed my life won't be too confusing.

The history of trauma in my life is broken into three separate sections: physical abuse, sexual abuse, and self-inflicted trauma.

Physical Abuse: What I Remember

The most vivid memories I have of my early childhood were the beatings by my father. How often he directed his anger and fury at me, slapping and punching me, knocking me off a chair, kicking me under the table when I tried to escape his wrath, and spanking me with what

139

ever was close at hand. Most of the physical abuse I endured came while my mom was away. My siblings and I were threatened into silence by fear of more punishments. We were not only fearful for our own

sakes, but for our mom. Because we loved the out-of-doors and were a pretty wild bunch who often displayed risky behaviour, bruises or injuries were easily explained away.

One of my earliest recollections of the fear I had of my father was during a walk in a park in Vancouver. I would have been three or four. I can't recall exactly what I did to raise his ire, but I must have known I was about to get another beating. I was crying and screaming as he dragged me into the bushes while he looked for a stick with which to mete out my punishment.

I can still hear the thwack and feel intense burning sensations across my back, hips, and buttocks. When he couldn't find his belt, supple willow branches or even hard, firm pieces of wood would suffice. To this day I can't remember what I ever did to justify such treatment.

On another occasion—one on which I can remember that I clearly misbehaved—he picked me up and threw me against the hall wall, causing my head to leave an indent in the plaster. What had I done? We had had family visiting with us. I would have been about five. And, as often happens when kids get together, we played and ran around the house making a lot of noise. Mom scolded us, demanding that we settle down. I came running around a corner and ran straight into my dad. And that's when he picked me up and threw me against the wall. I can't remember much of anything from that day. My father had no sense of proportion when it came to disciplining us. These kinds of events happened regularly – not always as serious, but definitely every day. It wasn't until I turned thirteen, when my father left us, that my beatings ended. What hurt me and impacted me far more than the beatings I got was seeing my siblings abused and mistreated by my father.

As I got a bit older and became more aware of the world and my surroundings, I developed a greater sense of empathy for my siblings. I became more acutely aware of my brother's and sister's hurts, and so I did my best to console them whenever they were unjustly punished, as they often were. And, as they got older, we would plan and strategize how we could avoid getting hurt.

We tried hiding, but we were found. We tried running away, but we were caught. We even tried hiding the disciplinary tools, especially the belt. This last attempt backfired big-time by infuriating Dad all the more. Our father was creative with his tools of torture, using at various times appliance cords, wooden spoons and spatulas, whatever might be *within arm's reach. The only way to truly escape Dad's fury was being out of the house. Being away from him was the only way to avoid being beaten and hurt. Avoidance worked best.*

By the time I was ten and Daniel five, we did our best to be out of the house. From spring to fall, we spent as much time as possible in the out-of-doors. All the while, we were afraid of telling Mom why we did what we did.

Our father was a deadbeat. He couldn't hold down a job and was as lazy as he was mean. Mom had to work to support the family. This was convenient for our father, as it meant there was little chance for Mom to catch him at his worst. What could I do?

When I was old enough to better understand the dynamics of our home environment, I felt compelled to do what I could to protect my brother and sister. From the time I was eight or so to when Dad left, I did whatever I could to distract our father to keep him from hitting or otherwise beating my siblings. I often took upon myself the punishment intended for them. Growing up in this kind of environment no doubt skewed our view of the world.

When my younger brother was about six, he met a twenty-two-year-old woman in the park where we played. She introduced herself and, knowing that he was alone for most of the day, invited him into her home for a meal. This became something of a daily routine. She appar-

ently liked to be called "Mom." I was about eleven when my brother introduced me to her. We became friends, and before we knew it, she had us stealing for her. We stole food from the corner/convenience stores, Canadian Tire, local businesses, and the grocery stores. "Mom" would feed us, give us a little money from the proceeds, and let us have the run of her apartment.

My brother and I soon branched out on our own. Risky behaviours were thrilling and rewarding, new and exciting experiences. My brother and I got into a number of things. We found out that there was an electronics warehouse in town and broke into it. I figured out how and when to go through coat pockets to steal purses and wallets at the local bowling alley. We had fun and money for weeks that summer, until we were caught.

Our real mom was none too pleased. Her children were now on police radar. Her reprimand, however, had little impact on our behaviour. Unlike our dad, she didn't beat us. We were just grounded and put to work to repay what we had stolen. We were not deterred, and our stealing escapades continued. Although Dad still meted out punishments whenever it suited him, now that the police had been involved he left Mom to deal with things like stealing. Thankfully, God soon intervened, closing a painful chapter in our lives.

When I was thirteen, our father openly declared that he was gay and that he would continue his homosexual activities. Mom would have no part of it and insisted that he leave. What he did next was for us so heinous that we planned to kill him. We saw him hit Mom.

Unfortunately, our risky behaviours continued unabated. To provide for us, Mom worked multiple jobs and long hours, leaving us to our own devices. Soon my brother and I parted ways. He continued with his stealing sprees, and I ran various cons and scams, trying to stay under police radar. We did not involve our sister in our respective enterprises, as we felt that she and Mom were the only wholesome things in our lives. I, on the other hand, was a runaway train. Could it get any worse?

In my early teens, I was confronted with a new foe—societal prejudice. In a small town of three thousand, my father's coming out and leaving his family caused me a very different kind of pain. I became an outcast, a pariah, ridiculed by my peers. I was taunted and often physically attacked. Girls regularly cast epithets and hurtful slurs at me, to the point that even today I am intimidated by females. Many observers turned a blind eye to my attackers.

I spent many days in detention for fighting. And, despite the fact that several teachers had pity on me, I could never fit in and never felt accepted. In order to survive, I had to give as good as I got, regardless of the size of my attacker. Most of them were much bigger than I was, but I learned to stand my ground.

In the summer after I finished grade 9, we moved in with my mom's new husband. He lived on a farm in a different county far away from my high school. I was saved; I could start over and be who I wanted to be, not what others thought of me. But my joy lasted only for that summer. To my horror, some of the most vile students from my former school were enrolled in my new school. Was I never to have relief?

As soon as they recognized me, two sisters from my former school started spewing their poison. Soon the bullying began in earnest. To avoid the bullies, I joined every club I could think of: the chess club, the debate club, the poetry club, the reading club, the math club, and even the BBS short for Bulletin Board System. Yes, I was online before the internet was up and running.

Unlike teachers from my former high school who had displayed disdain toward me, the teachers at my new school were gracious and kind. They were my saving grace. Their names are forever etched in my mind. I thank them for helping me survive my high school years. This was a special group of people, teachers who encouraged me and lifted me up. Not even the adults of my church had such a positive and meaningful impact on me. They quickly intervened whenever they saw me being bullied. They were the ones who encouraged me to join the various clubs. Still, life wasn't easy for me at school.

Whenever I was not actually in class or immersed in club activities and needed a safe haven to avoid the bullies, I would either hang with the smart kids in the library or with the stoner kids at the back of the school property. Although I was still harassed by some of the stoners from time to time, it was easier dealing with them than being in constant fistfights with the bullies.

I left high school early. I needed to "find myself." This is such a cliché, yet for me it was true without a doubt.

I believe that having had such a dysfunctional childhood, without a strong and loving father to help guide me, affected my decision making. I don't say this to excuse my mistakes, but rather to convey the difficulties and challenges faced by kids like me. It has long been understood and accepted that the healthy sexual development of a boy or girl is largely a consequence of the relationship they had with their fathers. In my case, I knew that I had a tough "row to hoe," as many of my choices were predicated on deep-seated issues brought on by the abuses that I had suffered. Even after many years, I'm still working through things.

Sexual Abuse: That Which Was Buried

At thirty-four, after three years of personal introspection undertaken in an attempt to leave behind the debauchery of my twenties, I went back to school, where I met the love of my life. Once we were married the kids came along fast and furious.

At forty, I was excited, anticipating the birth of our first child. In the fourth month of pregnancy, my wife and I went for her ultrasound to determine the sex of our child. Initially I was ecstatic and overjoyed to find out that we were going to have a boy, but soon thereafter my joy was overshadowed by a sudden fear and trepidation. The memories and pains of my childhood resurfaced: the terrible abuses at the hands of my father and his perverted friends; the abuses at the hands of a strange woman; the taunting in high school. Could I be a loving and caring father? Did I have what it took to be a good father? Would I be responsible enough to look after my wife and child? All these questions started to haunt me. In my confusion, I sought help. I needed counselling to help me make sense of what I was going through. Unfortunately, I was worse off after counselling than before.

What did I know of a father's love? Cuddling for a few minutes before I was violated yet again? What little remained of my self-esteem vanished, and in desperation I consciously began sabotaging my own life.

After my son was born on July 4, 2016, the pressure I felt became unbearable, and so I did what I had always done: I leaned on drugs to support me. I didn't need anyone's help. I could do it on my own. I stupidly thought that I could drown my emotions by living a lascivious life. I sought the company of women, even transgender women, for one-night stands, often paying for their services. How could this make any sense?

Self-Inflicted Trauma: The Identity Crisis

To help you better understand what led me to follow such a destructive course, I need to go back and fill in some blanks. I need to recall my destructive lifestyle from the time I left high school to my early thirties.

After high school, I often drove to Toronto. That's where the action was, and while on rare occasions I went there for work, it was most often for fun.

Through work, I met some very welcoming people in the LGBTQ community, and I was soon invited on outings with them. For the first time in my life, I had a sense of community and belonging. I was welcomed, and everyone seemed friendly, kind, and helpful. Right from the get-go I learned how they embraced drugs. I was in with the right crowd. I learned about all the hottest things on the party circuit. While in high school I had tried a bunch of drugs, including LSD, and so I was pretty open to trying new things. After all, I prided myself in being a risk-taker. And so I began experimenting with MDMA, cocaine, poppers, ketamine, and random psychedelics.

MDMA is what Aldous Huxley called "soma" in his book Brave New World. *Under its influence I felt euphoric—able, I thought, to accept and connect with everyone and everything in a relaxed calm. The only real side effect was a feeling of melancholy. And that to me was okay,* as when I was melancholy, I felt relaxed. For me, someone who struggled with poor self-esteem, MDMA helped me identify with my own sexuality—so I thought. Turbulent times were before me.

The third time that I took MDMA was at an after-hours club. Some of my friends—mostly gay men—and I were closing the place down. Sometime around five in the morning and high on the drug, I noticed an attractive woman leaning against the bar. We started a casual conversation, and before too long we were making out. We were both high.

Sometime later—I'm guessing it might have been about eight a.m.—one of my friends came over to me and asked me to step away to talk for a minute. To my shock he informed me that I was kissing a transgender woman, a biological male. Up to that point my romantic or sexual relations had only been with women. Stunned and confused, I left the bar. Was I truly a heterosexual or was my sexuality more fluid?

While I struggled with my feelings for a time, I shortly thereafter started dating both biological and transgender women. The confusion I had felt melted away as I continued taking and relying on MDMA. And, while I continued to struggle with my identity, drugs made it easy to dismiss my apprehensions, such as they were.

What I didn't understand—or care about, for that matter—were the dangerous side effects of MDMA. The drug was altering my thought processes, breaking down my ability to rationally make common-sense determinations. In my heart I knew that I was making a mistake trying to define my identity through sex, but the effects of the drugs, especially MDMA, blurred my thinking to the point where I convinced myself that, even though I continued this abhorrent lifestyle, I was truly a heterosexual. After all, even though I had sexual relations with biological men, my friends told me that I was indeed a heterosexual—or at worst, bisexual. Where did the truth lie? Was I lying to myself?

Contrary to the views of some of my friends who seemed convinced that my involvement with transsexuals didn't really alter the fact that I was straight, the destructive propaganda propagated by the LGBTQ community and supported by the left-wing media really messed me up. My torment was intense. Living this perverted lifestyle, all the while trying to hide it from my family, was killing me. I was so emotionally crippled that something had to change. Thankfully, in my state of despair something within me clicked.

I came to the realization that the path I was on would only end in tragedy. And, while I kept much of what I was doing secret, I could see it slowly destroying my family. Yet even in my confused state, I was blessed with a "still, small voice" inside me calling me back, back to what my mother had instilled in me as a child. If I was to save my family from complete ruin, I had to change the trajectory of my life. I had to choose right from wrong. But was I strong enough?

Epiphany: The Last Piece Falls into Place

About a year after the birth of my first son and during the time when I was struggling with MDMA, my wife became pregnant with our second son. While elated with the news, I was about to face the most heart-wrenching time of my life. I was paralyzed with fear as to what kind of father I would be. Would I—could I—do to my children what had been done to me?

No one knew the extent of my struggles, or the double life I had led for the past eight months. As the world seemed to collapse around me, I broke down and admitted to my wife and family what I had done. What I had known in my subconscious all along came to the fore. I had reached the point where I admitted to myself that I needed help. I needed support. I needed therapy to deal with the lingering consequences of my early childhood trauma.

Trauma is an insidious phenomenon. Sometimes its causes come to mind readily; at other times it lingers, hidden in the recesses. And, no matter how deeply it may be imbedded in our minds, it can suddenly and without warning come to the fore, triggered by environmental cues such as an event, interactions with others, a smell, or a taste. Although reminders of my early childhood trauma are waning, I deal with them to this very day. Only by the grace of God am I getting the help I need.

I was slowly able to move past my lustful desires for women and ef-feminate men and come to an appropriate appreciation of the female form. I have also come to appreciate the true meaning of self-worth, to embrace the qualities that truly identify who I am: things like God, faith, family, and good friends. I have a new awareness of how much I love my wife and family, and because of that, I understand my con-tinuing need for therapy. No more slipping back into debauchery. My mother and stepfather have been there for me, even when I might have "thrown in the towel." In her desire to help me, my siblings, and other trauma victims, my mother went back to school and now has a doc-torate in trauma therapy.

Today, my mother tours the country and beyond, speaking on the hor-rors of the sexualizing of our children. She has been the keynote speak-er at events as far away as Africa and more recently has been invited to tour the Caribbean. She is becoming a much sought-after lecturer, especially after the publishing of her second book, Closing the Flood-gates. *Most Canadian MPs have since been provided with a copy. Re-cently she asked me to join her in a meeting with several MPs to discuss the revelations in the book.*

29

Ruth, Chuck's Sister, Remembers

I am the third child and first girl in our family. My brother Chuck was ten years older than me. We were living in a city in southern Ontario when the abuse began. The first memories I had began when I was five years old.

When my parents went out, Chuck was often left to babysit my younger brother Ricky, my baby sister, and me. He would take us to the basement and make me play strip poker. One time, I remember him whipping my baby sister around in the basement while she was in her walker. He tossed her around so hard that she crashed into the metal beam in the center of the room, hitting her head. She cried for a long time, but it seemed to matter little to him. He was violent and aggressive.

Chuck's bedroom was next to our parents' room. He would wait until they were sleeping, then come into my room and take me back to his room to perform oral sex. He was absolutely brazen and, because of his threats, knew that I wouldn't tell.

Chuck also took me to a neighbour's where he and his friends would sexually abuse me and have sex with each other. Our family had moved back to my mom's hometown by this time, so I think I might have been six or seven. He and his friends sexually abused my siblings and me all the while that we lived there.

During this time, I befriended a girl on the street and would spend time at her house. Her father sexually abused her and soon started molesting me. We were just children. It seemed that I was surrounded by these pedophiles.

Chuck was not only a child molester; he was also a compulsive liar and manipulator. At the time of his molestations, he also began to steal from homes in the area. He'd have my younger brother crawl through a small window and then open the door for him to rob the home.

I think I was ten or eleven when we moved again, this time to a trailer park outside a nearby town. Chuck continued to molest me. It wasn't until I was about twelve and he was about twenty-two, when he married Ann, that it finally ended.

During the early years of my being molested, I tried to tell my mom. But she would look at me and tell me that it never happened. She was in complete denial. Chuck was her favorite and he could do no wrong. She most often took her anger out on the rest of us, hitting us with whatever was handy. I understand now what a dysfunctional family we were.

I met my future husband, Mark, in my late teens, and we have been married for nearly forty years. He has been my rock. Unfortunately Chuck, who despises him, has treated both of us horribly. Chuck constantly did his best to degrade me in front of Mark and others.

My dad only found out about the molestation of his children after Daniel came forward to disclose the abuse he had endured. After my sister disclosed the entire sordid affair to the police, she sent Dad a letter with the details of the sexual abuse she'd suffered at the hands of his eldest son. He was devastated.

Meanwhile my mother, in a feeble attempt to protect Chuck, continued in her denial. Dad, on the other hand, wept as he tried to console us. Years later, when on his deathbed, he shared the hope that he would see us all in heaven. Even then Chuck, in his narcissism and longing for attention, started to berate the rest of us in front of Dad. Chuck was as hurtful as he had ever been. It got so bad that he had to be escorted out of the hospital. What evil!

At Dad's funeral, things came to a head between Mark and Chuck. The family had gathered at the cemetery when Chuck began to spew his malice toward me. That pushed Mark over the edge, and he called Chuck out. Mark, a kind and quiet soul, had had enough. But did Mark's confronting Chuck in any way alter Chuck's behaviour? Not in the least. Just before our mother was admitted to a nursing home, Chuck demanded that she give him his inheritance. What bloody nerve! Anyway, was there anything left?

Since Ann's divorce from Chuck, he's gone from boyfriend to boyfriend in his sick and evil lusts. And while he has caused so much pain and suffering to so many of his family, he walked out of the courtroom acquitted. It still boggles my mind that the Crown attorney refused to hear our testimonies. Because only Daniel was asked to give his testimony, the presiding judge never heard the horrors the rest of us endured. Something just wasn't right about the entire trial. This, in my view, was a travesty, and I can't help but wonder how far and deep the evil of pedophilia runs in our society. It is no wonder that so many have such little faith in our justice system. Evil runs deep.

30

Ricky Speaks

I see a man coming into my room. He lives in our house, but he doesn't have a normal face—rather, that of a werewolf. I never really see his face. I just feel terror and panic as he comes for me. I can't grasp who it is. My mind just shuts out the face. He's a monster.

My brother is the monster. I can't see his face, but I know what he's doing to me. He's sodomizing me. My tears and pain mean nothing to him. It doesn't matter how I plead. I'm a kindergartner being raped.

It's been hard living with the reality of what happened to me in my childhood. I've lived with nightmares all my life. In these dreams, I want to run but can't. I'm not sure exactly when it all began, but much of what I do remember happened just after we moved to Mom's hometown.

My oldest brother, Chuck, would take me to a neighbour's house where he and a friend would take turns with me. They would have been about seventeen or eighteen at the time, and I was only six or seven. I had no choice. If I tried to run, they'd catch me and beat me. Other times, Chuck would bribe me with money to have sex with him and his friends. Chuck had a number of friends who were willing to participate. In particular, there was one really messed-up family of boys who lived a few miles from us. They all took part in the debauchery. Chuck went so far as to date one of the sisters to give the impression that he was straight. After one particularly horrific orgy, Chuck took me to the Canadian National Exhibition as a bribe in the hopes that I wouldn't tell anyone about being routinely sodomized.

Mom swallowed the lies hook, line, and sinker. When I tried to tell her what Chuck and his friends were doing to me, she shrugged it off. She wasn't about to admit that her son was a raving pedophile. "Just don't talk about it," she would say. What kind of mother does that? She was as evil as her oldest son. She was also cruel beyond words. If, in her anger, she wanted to beat us, she used whatever was close at hand. My scars tell the story.

The only reprieve was when we went fishing with Dad. He was good to us, but he worked long hours and would often go away on the weekends to escape Mom's wrath. She once threw an axe at him. Another time I saw her hit him with a cast-iron frying pan. Even though he was aware of her violent tendencies, he seemed oblivious to our circumstances during his absence. And we were too afraid to tell him about the sexual abuse and her treatment of us.

I have horrible memories of her vicious streak—like the time she threw boiling water over our female dog when a male came near her. I hated the fact that Mom acted so piously when at church. I hated her for it. And, although she dragged us to church, what good did going to church do for her? Why, then, should I bother with church? I didn't hate God, but my mom was another matter. What pained me the most weren't the beatings but rather her unwillingness to help me. Thinking about it, even today, brings me to tears.

After Chuck married Ann, he decided to go to Bible college to become a pastor. Mom was ecstatic as the rest of us watched from afar. Only after Daniel came forward did any of us make Ann aware of what had gone on during our childhood years. In fact, until Daniel's revelations, we didn't even talk about the abuses amongst ourselves. Had Ann known, she probably would not have married Chuck.

Given Chuck's evil, narcissistic, and selfish bravado, I have nothing to do with him today. Back when he and Ann were still married, I decided to live with them for a while in northern BC. Their children were still young, and I thought that if I was there, I could somehow protect them. Chuck got me a construction job that I really liked. But it wasn't long before he came on to me. He was disgusting. His lust was insatiable. He was carrying on with a guy at a Christian camp, a trapper. I couldn't stand it, and so I moved back to Ontario. I never told Ann about any of it. It was just too difficult. Looking back, I regret having been such a coward.

Daniel was brave to talk about it, but it had to cost him a lot emotion-
ally. After his story came to light, the police talked to each of us. Ruth,
Ruby, and I gave our testimonies individually. It was only then, when we
shared our stories with each other, that we learned that each one of
us had been molested by Chuck. We had all been intimidated by him
to keep quiet. We were confused when the Crown attorney only called
Daniel to testify. We weren't even allowed in the courtroom. I still can't
figure that out. It sure didn't make sense.

The judge never heard about all the children, including us, who had
been raped by Chuck since his early teens. To me, this was a case of
obstruction of justice by the Crown. Chuck got to walk! I can't help but
wonder if his connections to the gay community and their influence
behind the scenes had something to do with the acquittal. The victims
suffer forever with recurring traumatic memories, while this vile pred-
ator gets to walk. It seems to me that something was/is "rotten in the
state of Denmark."

Of us five siblings, only Ruth is still in her first marriage. She and Mark
have fought through the horrors and nightmarish memories and have
been able to deal with them. The rest of us, unfortunately, have had
tumultuous times in and out of brief relationships. There is no doubt in
my mind that the baggage we carry as a result of years of abuse has
caused us anxiety that will affect us for the rest of our lives. That said,
being able to finally talk about it is, to some extent, cathartic. One

could argue that we shouldn't let the past taint our current lives, but to them I would say that, unless someone has gone through what we've gone through, it's much easier said than done. It's a case of "walking in my shoes."

part three

THE GROOMING OF
CHILDREN

Within any important issue,
there are always aspects no one wishes to discuss.

GEORGE ORWELL

31

The Last Taboo

When the purpose of life and contentment is personal sexual freedom, there are no limits. Limits, boundaries, morality, are all considered to be expressions of suppression of sexual expression. But what happens in society when there are no limits and "too much is not enough"? [1] Let's take a look.

Pedophilia—the unspoken crisis we are now experiencing across nations.

What happens in your heart as you read that word? What do you feel? Does it stir you to anger, outrage, or tears? Perhaps you have no particular feeling about it. After all, it's just a word, right? But this word describes the primary desire of someone to have sex with children. For most, this word evokes strong negative reactions, and so it should. In general, the word refers to any sexual interest in children or the act of child sexual abuse by an adult.

The definition of pedophilia, taken from the Diagnostic and Statistical Manual of Mental Disorders, fifth edition, or DSM V[2] outlines specific criteria for use in the diagnosis of this disorder. Pedophilia is still both a mental illness classification as well as a criminal offence.

---

1   Swift, 1987
2   American Psychiatric Association, 2013

167

There are no typical pedophiles. They do not look different from other people. My ex-husband is a case in point: the "boy next door" kind of look, always ready to befriend children. These individuals don't carry signs declaring their deviance. They can be found in all professions, at all levels of society. They often hold respected and powerful positions in the community, and come from all racial and religious backgrounds. They are commonly related to or known by the victims or their family.

Pedophiles may act alone or organize themselves into groups which may operate within a local community, nationally, or internationally. In such groups, children and child pornography are passed between members. Such associations have gained momentum in recent years with the easy access of the Internet and the relative safety from exposure it brings.

Pedophiles are often very good at making friends with children quickly and can appear warm and approachable. They often come across as "nice men," which was a common description of my first husband. But these men are manipulative and sophisticated in how they attach themselves to families. Women pedophiles, while they exist, are still considered to be a rarity. Although the terms "grooming" and "pedophile" may be relatively new to some, the behaviour has been around for centuries.

Consider what the sexual revolution's hero, Alfred Kinsey, had to say in his 1948 study on boys and men, about the reactions of infants, as young as five months, and children who have been sexually violated (manipulated into orgasm):

- Extreme tension with violent convulsion
- Gasping, eyes staring
- Mouth distorted, sometimes with tongue protruding
- Whole body or parts of it spasmodically twitching

- Throbs or violent jerking of the penis
- Groaning, sobbing, or more violent cries
- Masochistic reactions (deriving sexual gratification from one's own pain or humiliation)
- Frenzied movements
- Extreme trembling
- Loss of color
- Fainting
- Pain or fright

Some subjects would fight to stay away from the "partner" (I would call it pedophile), making violent attempts to avoid climax.[3]

Kinsey's claim: "Homosexual masturbation of young boys is a valuable way to learn about childhood sexuality."[4]

This statement begs the question, heathy and beneficial for whom? Certainly not for the children who were left with lifelong emotional scars.

According to Kinsey, these are "typical cases" of the "orgasmic potential" of male infants and children. Let me say this again. Kinsey believed that these babies (some as young as five months) were displaying *orgasmic potential*.[5] Not so. On the contrary, these reactions are direct expressions of intense pain and suffering caused by masturbation and rape.

It was Alfred Kinsey who, in expanding on Freud's view of sexuality, advocated for early childhood sexuality and claimed that a

---

3   Reisman et al., 1990
4   Perry, 2003, p. 13
5   Perry, 2003

child is sexual from infancy onward. Kinsey's fraudulent "research" has inspired many academics to train educators to teach these concepts to even our youngest children.

Kinsey also said, "The only unnatural sex act is that which you cannot perform."[6]

Kinsey's assistant, Wardell Pomeroy, a successful academic, was a clinical psychologist who stated:

- "Incest between adults and younger children can also prove to be a *satisfying and enriching experience.*"
- "Incestuous relationships can—and do—work out well."
- "We find many beautiful and mutually satisfying relationships between fathers and daughters. These may be transient or ongoing, but they have *no harmful effects.*" [all emphasis mine][7]

While sexual abuse of children remains a repulsive act in the minds of the vast majority of people, pedophilia under the guise of "intergenerational intimacy" or "minor attracted persons" (MAPs) is gaining traction in our society due to a strong push from academia. The radicalization of terms and language is meant to soften the impact of the truth around the behaviour of pedophilia.

Here's the truth:

MAP	= pedophile
Sex with a minor	= rape
Underage woman	= child
Non-consensual sex	= rape

---

6   Kinsey, 1948
7   Pomeroy, 1976

Academics now claim that most MAPS first discover their attraction during puberty. These academics and MAPs believe that this attraction becomes a central part of their identity.[8] Remember the "born that way" mantra of the LGBT community? Prepare yourself for the new mantra of "pedophilic orientation."

Freimond (2009) suggests that MAPs with a same-sex attraction—homosexual desire for young boys—additionally experience a "second coming out" of sorts; they may identify as gay, then realize they are gay and have an attraction to minors.[9] MAPs often join online communities of like-minded individuals instead of coming out to people they know.[10] They are readily embraced in the LGBTQ community.

I challenge the idea that this behaviour is a central part of their identity. Addressing it as such is an attempt to integrate the "born that way" justification into the mainstream and therefore imply that practitioner/predators are not to be held accountable for their actions.

There are two intersecting types of sexual attraction I wish to discuss here: homosexual and pedophilic. I realize that equating these two terms will produce unease, but it should be no different than putting heterosexual and pedophilic in the same sentence.

The word "homosexual" describes someone who is attracted to the same sex, while "pedophile" describes an individual attracted to young children. A male homosexual pedophile, then, is someone who is generally, but not always exclusively, attracted to young boys. Pedophiles are nothing if not opportunistic.

---

8   Pedersen, 2017
9   Freimond, 2009; Goode, 2010
10   Goode, 2010; Freimond, 2009; Cash, 2016; Pedersen, 2017

Concerted attempts to separate homosexuality from pedophilia have been made for decades, claiming that pedophiles cannot, by definition, be considered homosexuals. The idea behind this is that pedophiles who molest boys cannot be homosexual if they have, at any time, been married or sexually involved with women. This is untrue; it is now a well-known fact that the vast majority of homosexuals have had sex with women at some point in their lives.

The re-engineering of the word "pedophilia" alone should be a wake-up call to parents. The terms "intergenerational intimacy" and "minor attracted persons" are attempts to downplay the horrible reality of childhood sexual abuse—rape. In fact, those who strive for the acceptance of adult–child sex deny the harsh reality of the physical pain and long-term mental anguish, so vividly described by Kinsey in 1948, that is suffered by the victimized children.

In 1991, academic Ken Plummer wrote, "Contemporary concern over pedophilia and child sexual abuse usually rests upon uncritical and under-theorized conceptions of childhood sexualities."[11] If this is confusing, Plummer goes on to say, "Pedophilia or *male intergenerational intimacy*" [I call it incest], uses the language of child love: consent, joy, willingness and choice—a language of desire."

Plummer declares, "...such love [*incest*] is in the best interests of the child.[12]

This view, according to Plummer, constructs a world of childhood where children are "naturally sexual" and adults may help them to joyfully explore their desires."[13]

---

11 Plummer, 1991, p. 231
12 Ibid.
13 Ibid.

Therefore, according to Plummer, society's concern over pedophilia and child abuse is basically because we don't know any better. Plummer would have us believe that parents need to stop being concerned, because such behaviour is perfectly normal, according to some academics.

Plummer is a gay academic who taught sociology for thirty years at the University of Essex. He openly advocates for adults to have sex with children. What some academics and pedophiles want the general public to believe is that *sexually abusing a child can be loving and kind* if they can mold the child into a sexual being as early as possible. This is what our public education system is actively doing.

In 2014, the *New York Times* ran an article called "Pedophilia: A Disorder, Not a Crime."[14]

In this report, the suggestion is made that we (society) think pedophilia is the same as child molestation. This article declares that pedophilia is not a choice, but rather a disorder that may have neurological origins—or, in simple words, pedophiles are "born that way," although there is no scientific basis for this suggestion. Of course, we've heard this phrase for more than forty years. It's the phrase that brought homosexuality into mainstream acceptance.

It may surprise you to know that there are groups which lobby and advocate for pedophilia, claiming it is a positive sexual experience. Such groups have been active since the 1950s.

Tom O'Carroll authored *Paedophilia: The Radical Case*[15] in 1980. O'Carroll claims that children's natural sexuality should not be

---

14   Kaplan, 2014; https://www.nytimes.com/2014/10/06/opinion/pedophilia-a-disorder-not-a-crime.html
15   O'Carroll, 1980

denied. In fact, to do so would be to cripple children. O'Carroll, like others before and since, advocates for pedophilic rights by muddying the waters to suggest that children will be less than fully developed—or worse, crippled—by not experiencing early childhood sex at the hand of adult males.

O'Carroll was a teacher who spent three years in the profession before coming into conflict with authorities over his declared love for one of his pupils, a boy aged thirteen.[16] He was imprisoned for conspiracy to corrupt public morals, the distribution of child pornography, and multiple convictions of sexual offences against children. But that didn't stop him for long. O'Carroll sat on the National Council for Civil Liberties sub-committee for gay rights[17] and for twenty years was the protégé of the UK National Council for Civil Liberties (NCCL, now Liberty).

We should be outraged at the "progress" pedophilic ideology has made within the LGBTQ community as well as society in general.

Here are a couple other organizations. According to the Wikipedia article on the North American Man/Boy Love Association,

> NAMBLA is a pedophilia and pederasty advocacy organization in the United States...founded in 1978. It works to abolish age-of-consent laws criminalizing adult sexual involvement with minors· and campaigns for the release of men who have been jailed for sexual contacts with minors that did not involve what it considers coercion. The group no longer holds regular national meetings, and as of the late 1990s—to avoid

---

16   Percy, n.d.; http://www.williamapercy.com/wiki/index.php?title=Tom_O%27Carroll_Biography

17   Bindel, 2015

local police infiltration—the organization discouraged the formation of local chapters.[18]

In reality there is little need in 2022 for local chapters, as the Internet provides unlimited access to like-minded individuals. I find it interesting that many who speak to societal issues are routinely censored by big tech, if they do not fall in line with their narratives. Yet these perverts, spewing their poison against our children unabated, are seldom censored. Is there no bottom to the depths of their depravity?

The Wikipedia article goes on to say,

> In December 1977, police raided a house in the Boston suburb Revere. Twenty-four men were arrested and indicted on over 100 felony counts of the statutory rape of boys aged eight to fifteen. Suffolk County district attorney...found the men had used drugs and video games to lure the boys into a house, where they photographed them as they engaged in sexual activity. The men were members of a "sex ring."

According to the district attorney, the arrest was "the tip of the iceberg."[19]

The Wikipedia article continues,

> The "Boston-Boise Committee," a gay rights organization, was formed in response to these events...allegedly in order to promote solidarity amongst gay men, saying in an official leaflet that: "The closet is weak.

---

18   "North American Man/Boy Love Association," Wikipedia, n.d.
19   Ibid.

There is strength in unity and openness." NAMBLA's founding was inspired by this organization...In 1994, ILGA [the International Lesbian and Gay Association] expelled NAMBLA.[20]

However, a Conservapedia article on NAMBLA states,

The International Gay & Lesbian Archives, the world's largest research collection on gay, lesbian, bisexual, and transgendered activism, has recognized several NAMBLA members for their contributions to the gay rights movement.[21]

According to Wikipedia, "NAMBLA was the largest group in International Pedophile and Child Emancipation (IPCE), an international pro-pedophile activist organization."[22] Wikipedia cites a newspaper report that says, "as of 2005...NAMBLA was based in New York and San Francisco."[23]

According to the IPCE website, the organization is "for people who are engaged in scholarly discussion about the understanding and emancipation of mutual relationships between children or adolescents and adults."[24]

Academic and social activist Camille Paglia joined the faculty at the University of the Arts in Philadelphia in 1984 and was a strong supporter of man/boy "love."[25] According to Wikipedia, "in 1994,

---

20   Ibid.
21   "North American Man/Boy Love Association," Conservapedia, n.d.
22   "North American Man/Boy Love Association," Wikipedia, n.d.
23   Ibid.
24   ipce.info
25   Paglia, 2014

Paglia supported lowering the legal age of consent to fourteen."[26]
She comments,

> These days, especially in America, boy-love is not only
> scandalous and criminal, but somehow in bad taste.
> On the evening news, one sees handcuffed teachers,
> priests and Boy Scout leaders hustled into police vans.
> Therapists call them maladjusted, emotionally imma-
> ture. But beauty has its own laws, inconsistent with
> Christian morality.[27]

Paglia also noted in a 1995 interview, "I fail to see what is wrong
with erotic fondling with any age."[28]

The Wikipedia article on NAMBLA states, "Gregory King of the
Human Rights Campaign" vehemently maintained that "NAMB-
LA is not a gay organization...they are not part of our community
and we thoroughly reject their efforts to insinuate that pedophilia
is an issue related to gay and lesbian civil rights."[29] Of course the
name NAMBLA by definition (man/boy love) is inescapably
homosexual.

In 2014 there was an attempt to reclassify pedophilia as a "sexual
orientation" in the Diagnostic and Statistical Manual of Mental
Disorders, fifth edition (DSM V).[30] Fortunately, there was enough
of a backlash that it prompted the American Psychiatric Association to issue a statement insisting the designation was in error.

Minor-attracted persons (MAPs) state they "often feel negatively

---

26 "Camille Paglia," Wikipedia, n.d.
27 Paglia, 1991
28 "Camille Paglia," Wikipedia, n.d.
29 Gamson, 1997
30 American Psychiatric Association, 2013

about themselves" due to "the stigma they face from society." Claims of "loneliness, distress, suicidal ideation, and low self-esteem are common themes, particularly for young MAPs coming to terms with their attraction for the first time."[31]

Words such as these are designed to tug at your heartstrings. Such claims cast MAPs as victims. This type of reframing has been part of the LGBTQ strategy since the 1970s. But the truth is that such individuals need not to be acknowledged, but rather to seek psychotherapy to deal with their twisted thoughts. Unfortunately, such therapy is now deemed abusive and will likely result in criminal charges against those who are equipped to help and who attempt to do so.

We need to be clear. Thoughts can make any of us feel negatively about ourselves. We each have a responsibility to rein in any thought that would cause us to feel negatively, especially sexual thoughts. It is our thoughts that fuel our emotions that in turn play out in our behaviour. It is the abused who are the true victims, not the one experiencing pedophilic thoughts and/or behaviour.

Since the 1970s we have learned a lot about the sexual abuse of children. The primary focus had historically been on the abuse of girls, and we must continue to be vigilant in our attempt to protect them. However, in more recent years, the increased incidence of sexual abuse among young boys has finally been exposed. David Finkelhor, the director of Crimes against Children in the U.S., states that one in five girls and one in twenty boys are victims of child sexual abuse (as reported to Child Services). But self-report studies show that 20% of adult females and 5% to 10% of adult males recall a childhood sexual assault or sexual abuse incident.[32]

31 www.b4uact.org/know-the-facts; Cacciatori, 2017; Cash, 2016; Vogt, 2006
32 Child Sexual Abuse Statistics, National Center for Victims of Crime

Other researchers believe that boys are sexually abused as commonly as girls.[33] One large study conducted by the U.S. Center for Disease Control found that the sexual abuse of boys was more likely to involve penetration of some kind, resulting in profound psychological harm.[34]

Speaking up about the abuse suffered as a child creates fear in the survivor. Will they be believed, if they tell? Will their parent(s) believe them? Will their teacher? Will the police? Will children's services? And what happens next? It's an ongoing continuum of doctor's appointments and investigations. If a parent is the offender, what will that mean for the child and for the other parent? And, while the rape of a child by a parent is labelled as incest rather than pedophilia, is it much of a stretch to believe that such a predator can do the same to any child?

A case study by the British Columbia Institute against Family Violence declared that in 80% of sexual abuse occurrences, the sex offenders occupied community positions of trust. These male sex offenders were often well-known and respected for their work with children, and were most often fathers. In the remaining 20%, offenders were friends and/or neighbours of the victims.[35]

Consider the recent $850 million financial settlement involving the Boy Scouts of America in which "tens of thousands" of boys claimed that they had been sexually abused. This was the largest settlement "in a child sexual abuse case in United States history." Most of the victims of these crimes, now in their 60s and 70s, were in their teens when they were abused. "More than 84,000 individuals" were "part of the lawsuit against the 110-year-old organization" which, since the 1960s, had been "plagued with claims

---

33   MacFarlane et al., 1986

34   Hopper, n.d.

35   Barrier, n.d.

of abuse from volunteers and leaders." The article goes on to state that "the Boy Scouts of America filed for Chapter 11 bankruptcy last year as it faced mounting legal costs."[36]

Many men who are attracted to the same sex are, like my ex-husband, in heterosexual marriages, not identifying as LGBT. I believe that there is an undeniable correlation between homosexuality and the sexual abuse of boys. If homosexuality can be presented as a healthy, good, and normal "lifestyle" in the face of overwhelming evidence to the contrary, so can pedophilia. This normalization of perversion is exactly what is on the horizon. Children are being groomed in schools and in social media to accept pedophilic interests.

We know that child sex offending (CSO) has disastrous effects on children's mental well-being and development that persists into adulthood[37] and may lead to structural and functional changes in children's brains.[38, 39] For more on this see my book *Closing the Floodgates: Setting the Record Straight on Gender and Sexuality* (Gillies, 2017).

Children rarely behave in a highly sexual manner unless they have been groomed or conditioned to do so. To say our children are sexual from infancy is a lie. The sad thing is that children are now actually being "groomed" in classrooms to believe this.

The level of harm and the long-term effects caused by sexual abuse depend largely on such things as the abuser's identity, the duration of the abuse, whether the child confided in anyone at the time of the abuse, and whether they were believed and subsequently helped through the healing process.

---

36 Siegel, 2021
37 Kessler et al., 2010
38 American Psychiatric Association, 2013
39 Seto, 2017

Kevin Kantor described how it felt to see his rapist on social media. In the video link cited in the reference section, he passionately describes his reactions. "No one comes running for young boys who cry rape," he says.[40]

---

40   Kantor, 2015

32

Porn & Pedos

Let me introduce my colleague, therapist Jon Uhler. Jon is a licenced professional counsellor (LPC), a certified clinical trauma professional (CCTP), and a certified sex offender treatment professional. Jon is also founder and director of Survivor Support;[41] founder of the Church Project;[42] author of the Survivor Support blog;[43] and host of *Journey to Healing*.[44] He not only has the academic training, but also the extensive experience to speak of the issues of pedophilia and use of pornography.

Jon began his career treating survivors of sexual abuse for many years before extending both his training and his practice to sexual offenders. His time working with sexual offenders in the prison system makes him well qualified for addressing "porn and pedos" in this chapter. His firsthand knowledge of the correlation between pornography and pedophilia should have us soberly re-evaluating the laws on pornography. Jon wrote the following, and has graciously given me permission to include it in this book. Read his words carefully.

---

41   http://SurvivorSupport.net)
42   http://ChurchProtect.org
43   http://SurvivorSupport.US
44   http://TECNTV.com

My perspective as a therapist regarding the key contributing factors and influences that lead men to become sexual predators had been challenged by the late Dr. Judith Reisman, Ph.D., and her book Kinsey: Crimes and Consequences.

It was Dr. Reisman who uncovered how the fraudulent and criminal research of Dr. Alfred Kinsey was used to open the door toward normalizing sexual deviance and decreasing criminal penalties for sexual offenses. Kinsey as well played a key role in influencing Hugh Hefner to launch Playboy, thus giving birth to the pornography industry.[45] *Gillies (2017) gives a detailed account of Kinsey's activities in her book* Closing the Floodgates: Setting the Record Straight on Gender and Sexuality.[46]

I was also challenged through the death row interview between James Dobson, Ph.D., and serial killer Ted Bundy.[47] *Dr. Reisman's work and Dr. Dobson's interview would prove to be seminal in my thinking regarding the role pornography plays in men progressing into sexual deviance. When I began working with sex offenders in the prison system, I began looking into the extent to which pornography was associated with sexual offending.*

After years of working with sexual offenders, I acquired the unique ad-

---

45   https://www.thereismaninstitute.org/reisman-articles/2021/1/27/mkul-tra-kinsey-amp-rockefeller

46   Gillies, 2017

47   https://www.youtube.com/watch?v=_r2XzTcVaW4

vantage afforded a psychology staff member within a prison setting. This afforded me access to the offender's entire adult and juvenile criminal histories (juvenile histories are sealed from the public, but not from those on prison psych staff); all of their mental health records prior to prison; any pertinent school behavioral adjustment records; any and all prior involvement with social services; county probation; all written correspondence the inmate receives; all phone calls made; what he reads and watches on TV; what he has in his room and in his belongings; and the ability to verify and corroborate what the inmate discloses with others outside the prison system.

I was also able to obtain information of offenders on parole as to their whereabouts and associations, and what is on their cell phones can be monitored and reviewed.

Having reviewed hundreds of criminal histories and interviewed thousands of men who have sexually offended, I am able to confidently assert that there is a 100% correlation between pornography and men who offend sexually. In other words, 100% of men who perpetrate sex offenses will have been found to have been progressively accessing pornography for years prior to committing their sex offense. Additionally, 100% of all those men who have sexually offended a child will be charged with the possession of child pornography. Nearly all of the men with child victims will also be charged with the distribution/dissemination of child pornography as well.

I began to take a serious look into the correlation between pornogra-phy and offending. My specialized treatment unit within a long-term solitary confinement environment, and also on the regular solitary confinement units, allowed me to accrue more clinical contact hours than any other therapist. I was also involved in many sex offender groups (both high and low intensity) and spent a year overseeing the clinical treatment of one of the sixty-five-bed specialized sex offend-er treatment units for the Pennsylvania Department of Corrections. The specialized sex offender treatment unit was designed to provide treatment for men deemed to be high risk and/or SVPs (sexually violent predators). More recently, I have been running sex offender treatment groups for sex offenders on parole.

Since the advent of pornography and the Internet, I've found that sex offending is always accompanied by the influence of pornography in the life of the sexual perpetrator prior to his committing a sex offense.

During my eleven-plus years on psychology staff; conducting years' worth of sex offender treatment groups; hundreds of parole psycho-logical evaluations and countless sex offender risk assessments as well as sex offender treatment evaluations, I also began to see a clear cor-relation between the kinds of sexual offenses, the degree of deviance, the level of risk, and the kind of pornography the offender had progres-sively accessed by the time of their arrest. The progression and kind of pornography accessed by men who had progressed into pedophilia and child offending was deviant to the extreme. The knowledge I have is based upon the offenders' self-reports and actual police reports contained in criminal files.

Most academics who are now who are producing "peer reviewed" findings downplaying the role of pornography in offending[48, 49, 50] have spent precious little time with sex offenders behind bars where the real truths of sexual predators will reliably and verifiably emerge.

Following are some of the charts[51] I developed showing the progressive relationship of pornography, deviance, and offending.

---

48 Pornography Use and Sexual Offending: An Examination of Perceptions of Role and Risk - PubMed (nih.gov)
49 Sexual Abuse: Pornography and Contact Offending (atsa.com)
50 Sexual Abuse: Pornography and Contact Offending (atsa.com)
51 Uhler, 2022. Private correspondence

THE RANGE OF SEX OFFENSES CATEGORIES & THE MORAL DISPOSITION OF KINDS OF SEX OFFENDERS

THE RANGE OF SEX OFFENDERS

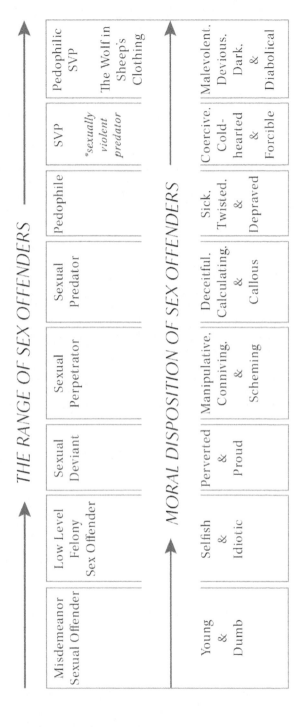

MORAL DISPOSITION OF SEX OFFENDERS

Misdemeanor Sexual Offender	Low Level Felony Sex Offender	Sexual Deviant	Sexual Perpetrator	Sexual Predator	Pedophile	SVP	Pedophilic SVP
						sexually violent predator	The Wolf in Sheep's Clothing
Young & Dumb	Selfish & Idiotic	Perverted & Proud	Manipulative, Conniving, & Scheming	Deceitful, Calculating, & Callous	Sick, Twisted, & Depraved	Coercive, Cold-hearted & Forcible	Malevolent, Devious, Dark, & Diabolical

HOW DIFFERENT ARE THEY FROM "REGULAR" SEX OFFENDERS?

RANGE OF SEX OFFENDERS

Misdemeanor Sexual Offender	Low Level Felony Sex Offender	Sexual Perpetrator	Sexual Deviant	Sexual Predator	Pedophile	SVP*	Pedophilic SVP

Personality Disordered

Profoundly Sexually Twisted, Warped & Deviant

Driven by Sexual Gratification via Power & Control

Actively Seeks to Sexually Defraud & Steal

Victim Unable or Unwilling to Consent

Meets Criteria for Pedophile

Dominance & Degradation

No Empathy or Conscience

Desire to Generate Trauma

Desire to Defile Children

*SVP is the acronym for sexually violent predator.

THE PROGRESSION OF SEXUAL DEVIANCE

Prolonged Attraction & Emotional Pull	Leaving one's self open to temptation (No Personal Firewall)	Actively allowing sexually provocative or stimulating material	Seeking out sexually stimulating material	Seeking out graphic sexually stimulating and explicit material	Sexually Exploitative or degrading material, using SBDM. Bi/Tri-sexual, Erotica (50 Shades of Gray)	Sexual use, manipulation, exploitation, & degradation of youth.	Calculated sexual rape and use of children for purposes of personal power & control, sexual deviance, profit, and ego-satisfaction at having defrauded their innocence.	Cold, calculated methodical, & strategic raping of the child or adult.
		Eg. S/I, Victoria Secret Catalogue, Explicit Romance Novels	*Eg. Soft-core porn such as Playboy*	*Eg. Hustler, Penthouse*	*Computer simulated alter-egos, animal character, anime, photographing*	Sexual degradation and violence of adults. CI detective stories, SBCM with minors, photographing for profit, beastiality.	Sexual violence against adults. Silence is secured by threats of harm or death of their victim or his/her family.	Motivated by: the "thrill of the chase," "cat & mouse," the ability to fool those who would try to stop him, and permanently defiling, traumatizing, terrorizing, dehumanizing, & destroying the victims.
						Bribes and "secrets" are used to gain the victim's silence.		

THE PROGRESSION INTO DARK SEX & PEDOPHILIA

1. *He Has become comfortable with immoral and depraved sensuality.*
2. *He gives himself over to pornography (soft-core pictures, hard-core pictures & videos, chatrooms, erotica, "barely legal," fantasy/role play, SBDM, homosexual-themed, detective/CI, child porn, bestiality, torture).*
3. *He willfully deviates into perverse, the forbidden, and taboo porn and activities*
4. *He descends into domination of his partner.*
5. *He descends further into power & control.*
6. *He sexually violates a non-consenting minor.*
7. *He descends even further into a desire to steal purity and innocence.*
8. *He descends still further to degrade.*
9. *He desires to mar and deface, steal & destroy.*
10. *He sexually offends a child in any way possible, being willing, able, and finding pleasure in the victim's trauma*

These charts illuminate the truth of porn progression and for me (Ann) depict explicitly the dark reality of life with a pedophilic sexually violent predator such as the one my children and I experienced. He was indeed the "Wolf in Sheep's Clothing."

Our society now readily accepts pornography as a normal activity, even to the point of enthusiastically encouraging its use. For survivors of violent sexual abuse this is not just a slap in the face but akin to being systematically re-abused.

Our culture has travelled so far down the rabbit hole of sexual immorality that we can no longer ascertain good from evil.

33

Bestiality

The term "bestiality" is used to describe the use of animals for human sexual gratification. I am broaching this topic as it goes hand in hand with child pornography and pedophilia. If you think that bestiality is something inconsequential and rare, you are woefully misinformed. Perversions such as this are on the rise exponentially. As proof, the arrest of these predators is becoming an ever-increasing occurrence.

Just as children have been used for the sick pleasure of their abusers, so too have animals. Unfortunately, reports involving animals are viewed as less important; they are less frequently investigated or prosecuted.

This issue came to light in our home in 1978. It was only after Chuck's three-day escapade with his gay buddies that this fact hit home. Upon his return, the anxiety felt in our home was palpable. He explained to me that he and a friend had traveled to Bellingham, Washington, where they discovered a new perversion, bestiality.

Chuck described a group who had experimented having sex with animals, especially dogs. They also had sex with goats and larger farm animals. I was appalled, and my look of disgust shut him up.

Even then, I didn't make the connection in my mind that Chuck was doing more than actually witnessing this.

Deviant and abhorrent behaviour is not confined to any particular group or segment of society. It is not a respecter of persons. It is everywhere. As I was writing this chapter, I came across a report that again shows how deviant individuals are so adept at hiding their evil side—under the guise of caring, no less. Veterinarians in most areas are required to report suspected animal abuse. But what if it's the vet himself who is the perpetrator?

The United States Attorney's Office, Southern Districts of Florida, identified a well-educated and trusted individual who used his position and occupation as a place to practice his dominance and repulsive sexual behaviour. In March of 2021, a well-known veterinarian was charged with child porn, "animal crushing," and having sex with dogs. Prosecutors "charged 40-year-old Prentiss K. Madden with receiving and possessing child pornography and with animal crushing, a federal crime."[52]

> Law enforcement agents received a Cyber Tip that an IP Address registered to Madden's home in Miami repeatedly accessed a cloud-based file-sharing service containing images of *child pornography*. As part of the investigation, law enforcement agents executed a search warrant on Madden's home....Agents also discovered over *1000 images* of child pornography and animal abuse in Madden's cloud-based sharing account, says the court filing [emphasis mine]....The criminal complaint charges Madden with one count of child pornography...one count of possession of child

52   www.justice.gov/usao-sdfl/pr/aventura-veterinarian-charged-federal-child-exploitation-and-animal-abuse-crimes

pornography...and one count of animal crushing.[53]

As gruesome as it is to explain, "crushing" is a reality. It is known as a paraphilia, a sadistic arousal by either committing or watching the crushing of small objects or small animals like kittens or rabbits.

According to the *New York Post*, "Veterinarian Prentiss Madden (Caring Hands Animal Hospital) was sentenced to 272 months in prison after he plead [*sic*] guilty to child pornography and animal cruelty charges."[54]

The Prevent Animal Cruelty and Torture (PACT) Act was signed by President Donald Trump in 2019, and then unanimously passed in the U.S. House and Senate. Now those who commit the most heinous acts of animal abuse—including crushing, burning, drowning, suffocating, and impaling animals—will face federal prosecution. Finally. Justice.

In the 1960s, a team of researchers compared incarcerated males, convicted male sex offenders, and a control group of non-incarcerated males using various metrics. The overall finding was that, among the 2,715 people studied, 17.7 percent of the sex offenders, 14.7 percent of the prison inmates, and 8 percent of the control group reported had committed sex acts with animals.[55]

Nearly forty years passed before another study was conducted involving convicted sex offenders and their sexual behaviour with animals. Three studies were published between 2003 and

---

53   Ibid.
54   Florida vet Prentiss Madden sentenced for sexually abusing dogs, storing child porn (nypost.com)
55   Gebhard et al., 1965

2008.[56, 57] On average, 43 percent of sex offenders reported having had sex with animals, a considerable increase since the sixties.[58]

Abel and Harlow (2009) report that bestiality arrests in the United States have gone from 3 between 1975 and 1980 to 259 between 2011 and 2015 (emphasis mine). Among child sex offenders, when compared with other reported deviant behaviours such as exhibitionism, frotteurism, and addiction to pornography, bestiality was found to be the single most important factor in predicting the potential risk of an individual molesting a child, particularly if sexual contact or interest in animals began at an earlier age.[59]

Here we see a trilogy—homosexuality, pedophilia and bestiality. It's time for the worms to come out of the woodwork.

In a 2016 study of 150 adult animal cruelty offenders, 12 men arrested for abusing animals sexually had also sexually abused and assaulted people where more than half of their victims had been under the age of 18.[60]

If after reading this chapter you felt defiled, I understand. As the author, I too felt defiled, and the more I delved into the subject, the more nauseating it became. Nevertheless, this unadulterated evil must be exposed, which brings me to one of the most distressing factors—the sexualizing of our children in schools.

56   English et al., 2003
57   Simons et al., 2008
58   Edwards, J., 2019
59   Abel and Harlow, 2009
60   Levitt et al., 2016

34

Unmasking Homosexuality

It has been an emotional journey for me as I have listened to my children's and Chuck's siblings' horrific stories. And if I had not spent years in education pursuing degrees and years in private practice helping individuals who had suffered sexual abuse as children, I don't think I could have listened to it all and kept my sanity.

What I have come to realize is that the abusing and sexualizing of our children has its roots in movements that began decades ago. Although there's been a movement to sexualize our culture since the 1860s, it hit its stride with the sexual revolution of the sixties, then the homosexual revolution of the seventies and eighties, followed by the LGBTQ revolution. This will be a very unpopular topic to some, but this agenda must be exposed for what it is so we can be prepared for the dangers we face if we do not curtail its permeation through society. Listen to some of the words written by gay activist Michael Swift in "The Gay Revolutionary" (1987; all emphasis mine).[61]

- The family unit—spawning ground of lies, betrayals, mediocrity, hypocrisy and violence—will be abolished.
- We shall sodomize your sons.
- They will be recast in our image.

---

61   Swift, 1987

- Women, you say you wish to live with each other instead of with men. Then go and be with each other. We shall give your men pleasures they have never known.

- Our writers and artists will make love between men fashionable and de rigueur, and we will succeed because we are adept at setting styles.

- We will eliminate heterosexual liaisons through usage of the devices of wit and ridicule, devices which we are skilled in employing.

- We are everywhere; we have infiltrated your ranks.

- All churches who condemn us will be closed. Our only gods are handsome young men. We adhere to a cult of beauty, moral and esthetic. All that is ugly and vulgar and banal will be annihilated.

- We are free to live our lives according to the dictates of the pure imagination. For us too much is not enough.

- We shall rewrite history.

Although Swift made claims that "The Gay Revolutionary" was intended to be satire,[62] his words ring true. Our sex-positive culture has arrived at the very place Swift prophesied about in 1987. Surely "they" are everywhere: in every place of learning, from day care to university; in every government institution and professional association; in every film, sitcom, and advertisement.

According to Swift, too much sex, influence, or propaganda is never enough. Crushing all limits of sexual expression and behaviour is the goal. Opening the floodgates of pedophilia and the annihilation of humanity is the result.

---

62   https://sourcebooks.fordham.edu/pwh/swift1.asp

35

Sex Education, Pornography, & the Grooming of Our Children

Sex ed curriculum revisions have been taking place at breakneck speed for two generations. With the overhaul of our sex education curricula over the last twenty years with the focus on sex, sex, sex, we are witnessing a dramatic increase in child molestation, even children against other children. Children are being groomed in the classroom to serve the interests of pedophiles, just as adolescent boys in ancient Rome were to satisfy the insatiable desires of adult men. This is not say that the vast majority of teachers, professors, and scholars are themselves pedophiles—which they are not—but rather that those who draft new curricula have their own agenda and know exactly what they're doing. History is being repeated. It has been said that if we don't learn from history, we're bound to repeat it. Unfortunately, the human condition over millennia has not changed. We must be vigilant and assertively protect our children.

My prayer is and has been that parents will awake to the danger. They are—or should be—their kids' first and primary educators. We cannot relinquish that responsibility to others, be they teachers or caregivers. The good news is that many have come to that realization.

In 2021, the mayor of Hudson, Ohio, called for the resignation of the entire Board of Education after high school seniors were assigned a controversial book with writing assignments that asked them to describe sexual experiences, to pretend they were serial killers, and other nefarious suggestions.[63]

At that time, board president David Zuro responded that none of the board members had "indicated any intention to resign."[64] Situations such as this are why concerned parents need to take back control of school boards.

The assignment that sparked the mayor's strong reaction was a book titled *642 Things to Write About.* The book contains prompts such as:

- Describe your favorite part of a man's body using only verbs.
- Write a sex scene you wouldn't show your mom.
- Write a sermon for a beloved preacher who has been caught in a sex scandal.
- Describe a time when you wanted to orgasm but couldn't.
- Ten euphemisms for sex.
- Write an X-rated Disney scenario.
- A roomful of people who want to sleep together.
- The first time you had sex.[65]

---

63   Burke, 2021
64   Ibid.
65   https://www.cleveland.com/akron/2021/09/hudson-mayor-craig-shubert-parents-call-for-resignation-of-hudson-school-board-teachers-after-students-receive-book-of-inappropriate-writing-prompts.html

The article also stated that Erik Dirker, a local police officer who attended the meeting, "called for the school to install cameras in classrooms at the board meeting."

Now there's a great idea. Instead of spending millions on LGBTQ inclusion material and pornographic books for children as young as five, let's demand accountability for what is being taught.

In speaking of LGBTQ inclusion, we must not leave out the push to have our children identify as transgender. My friend and colleague Jon Uhler, founder of SurvivorSupport.net, says this:

> A key red flag indicator of a possible, if not likely, sexual predator is *any* adult who is eager to gain direct access to your child, and who focuses on their sexuality, sex, and gender. Where do you find the greatest collection of such adults? Anywhere you find adults pushing the "Trans Deception."[66]

Parents, grandparents, teachers, pastors, politicians, and all leaders need to awake to the atrocities happening under our noses, in the guise of an "equality and anti-bullying" strategy. While equal rights and anti-bullying are always important to consistently respect, the pendulum has swung so far that our children now regard their parents as the enemy.

Publicly educated children and "progressively minded parents" have an entirely different set of values and assumptions than what was considered normative development a mere decade ago.

The presence of gender ideology that touts boys' bathrooms

---

66   Uhler, 2022. Private correspondence

dispensing tampons,[67] and a recently released video of a purported U.S. Department of Education training session featuring a biology teacher claiming, "I would say, no, it's not women that produce eggs. It's ovaries that produce eggs"[68] are just a couple examples of the progressive posturing and deception that is taking place in our public schools.

If you are interested in the transgender phenomenon—and you should be—please visit my website at www.restoringthemosaic.ca for more in-depth information.

Arise, parents! It's time to take back our school boards and the education of our children. It's well past time to rescue our children from a pedophilic agenda that would love nothing more than to groom our children by desensitizing them.

---

67 https://nypost.com/2022/05/06/oregon-law-requires-menstrual-products-in-boys-bathrooms/

68 https://www.foxnews.com/media/libs-of-tiktok-teacher

part four

ONGOING ABUSE IN MODELLING, MUSIC & FILM INDUSTRIES

36

Mommas, Don't Let Your Girls (or Boys) Grow Up to Be Models

Let me introduce you to Marrite, who has graciously agreed to let me share her story here. She is an absolutely beautiful and delightful woman, now in middle age, who has a quite a story to tell. She spent her successful career using her keen eye for beauty to develop new models—including supermodels. She gives the following account of the underworld of modelling.

Marrite began her own modelling management business at the age of twenty-one. She was a young woman of vision and passion. Her passion was to scout for models. Marrite "discovered" models. She had an eye for the unique, the special, and the ones who would excel in the career of modelling. Marrite had a gift to cheer everyone on, a gift of recognizing the beautiful.

Marrite discovered supermodels who skyrocketed to the top of the international modelling world. Her models worked all over the world, and she traveled the world in search of them. Marrite had stories featured in *Elle, Flare* magazine, *Teen Vogue,* the *New York Times*, and many others. She made many television appearances and even hosted her own television show called *Supermodels*.

Modelling was her life, and it became the life of the young girls she discovered. As a modelling agent she was invited backstage, where she started to see things that greatly disturbed her. She had to put her head in the sand in order to excel in business—and she did, for over two decades.

These young teens were naïve, vulnerable, and impressionable. Cocaine, the "skinny drug," was readily available, and young girls were encouraged to participate. The girls were groomed by rich men, who displayed an attitude that said, "Once they get the drugs into them, the girls will do anything." These men would gain their trust, then seduce them.

As she tells her story, tears well up. In the industry she was called the mother hen. Marrite tried her best to protect her "girls" and discouraged them from getting involved in drugs and in pursuing the advances of men more than twice their age. The girls lived in the public world of celebrity culture and corporate deceit.

While she protected, other agents lured the girls, grooming them by gaining their trust with lavish dinners, expensive clothing, and promises of stardom, then introducing them to rich men such as Jeffrey Epstein, who then used them as sexual toys, discarding them at whim.

Male models were not exempt from sexual grooming. Most of the stylists were gay. While the girls saw them as harmless, young male models were preyed upon. Drugs lowered inhibitions toward gay sex.

> Modelling is a business particularly predisposed to excesses. Supplying rich men with underage models was a chunk of the business I wanted no part of.

> I remember attending an extravagant dinner where

Jeffrey Epstein's friend, modelling agent Jean-Luc Brunel, was holding court. Of all the people I met, I found him the creepiest of all the agents I ever dealt with. I didn't send any of my girls to him.

In February of 2022, Jean-Luc Brunel was found hanged in his cell in La Santé prison in Paris. He had been "held for over a year as he was investigated on suspicion of the rape of minors and trafficking of minors for sexual exploitation."[69]

His arrest was part of a French inquiry into sex trafficking and sexual assault allegations against Epstein, focusing on potential crimes committed against French victims and suspects who are French citizens. Prosecutors suspected Brunel of raping, sexually assaulting and sexually harassing multiple minors and adults. They also suspected him of transporting and housing young girls or young women for Epstein.[70]

As Marrite told me this story, she said, "His arrest was of no surprise to me…Neither was his death, nor the suspicious claim that he killed himself. I don't believe that for a minute. I believe he, like Epstein, was murdered in order to keep the dark truth of the modelling business silent."

The underbelly of modelling, Hollywood, the music industry, is now being uncovered for what it really is—a hotbed of corruption and a means for mining our most precious, our children and youth, and funneling them into the hands of predators for sexual pleasure and exposure to the darkest perversions.

---

69   https://www.bbc.com/news/world-europe-60443518
70   Ibid.

37

The Music & Film Industry

Anthony Edwards, widely known for his role as Dr. Mark Greene on the series *ER*, is also a child sexual abuse survivor. He was molested by Hollywood producer Gary Goddard.[71] Anthony reveals:

> I met Goddard when I was 12, and he quickly became a dominant force in my life. He taught me about the value of acting, respect for friendship, and the importance of studying. Pedophiles prey on the weak. My father, who suffered from undiagnosed PTSD from WWII, was not emotionally available. Everyone has the need to bond, and I was no exception. My vulnerability was exploited. I was molested by Goddard; my best friend was raped by him—and this went on for years. The group of us, the gang, stayed quiet.

Sexual Favours Expected

A couple of years ago, I (Ann) met a famous musician who, on condition of anonymity, shared his experiences in the world of entertainment.

---

71   Edwards, A., 2017

I sang before the Queen, government leaders, and with such stars as Celine Dion. I know the music industry well. It is filled with alternative lifestyle folk. I am not homophobic, transphobic, or racist, but I am willing to speak about what I have seen.

My first experience of heterosexual prejudice came from a famous vocal coach: "You have a beautiful voice, but you'll never have a career; you're not gay." My first music professor was gay. He was a super friendly guy who was very touchy feely. He made me feel extremely uncomfortable. He was a nice guy, who engaged and managed artists. I was secure in my masculinity and sexuality, so I thought I'd be able to ward off sexual advances, which I was able to do, to the jeopardy of my career.

In 2003 I auditioned with twenty-eight others in Philadelphia at the American Vocal Arts Academy. There was one other man there who was married. When the accompanist looked at my wedding ring, he gave an exaggerated sigh.

I subsequently met another male vocalist who told me he never wears his wedding ring, because "they" (the music establishment) only want gay or willing. They like to audition on the couch. He also said I'd have a much bigger career if I gave in to the gay culture. Sexual favours are expected.

Finally in 2008 I received a contract on the spot at a national casting call and my journey to the abyss began. My manager and his gay partner would regularly take a few of us to dinner, where he would hit on young underage boys who were cleaning tables. Both men were continuously flirty. I was very disturbed by what I was seeing, but everyone just laughed it off with an "Oh, well!"

My manager talked of big parties with legendary actors where young boys would be brought in for pleasure. Many of these stars were married with children. The higher I ascended in the music industry, the more perversion I saw. In 2012 a billionaire in Nebraska wanted to meet our group for the purpose of investing. This billionaire helped fund an organization that gives millions of dollars for scholarships for "at risk" youth. At fundraising events older men would be surrounded by young boys. Hardly any women were ever present.

Another popular event was a "boys club." Here they held mock coronations. A "king," usually in his seventies or eighties, would be crowned; then they would bring in a "queen," a fourteen-year-old girl. We were asked to serenade at the tables where presidents and past presidents were seated. I had previously looked up to these individuals as distinguished governmental leaders, but when I saw sex between adults and children encouraged, I quickly changed my mind.

By 2014 I really began to see things for what they really were. When I saw the stars ogling young boys and the rest of the band saying "Just ignore it," I wanted to say something. But I had noticed that individuals that spoke out and accused stars and industry leaders of sexual molestation seemed to suddenly die after such disclosures.

I challenged my band with the idea of receiving funding from child trafficking groups, which of course was not well received, as you can imagine. The more venues we played, the more corruption I was exposed to. I began to investigate some organizations and found that highly qualified individuals had been investigating sex rings and following the money. One man in particular drew my attention.

Ted Gunderson, an FBI agent for 27 years, "retired as Special Agent-in-Charge with 700 agents under his command and a budget of $22.5 million. Then, as an independent investigator, he ran smack-dab into the grotesque business of blackmail, extortion, frame-up and cover-up."[72]

Gunderson exposed the Franklin child abuse cover-up. State senator John DeCamp has written about these atrocious events, and subsequent dismissal of witnesses' testimony, in his book *The Franklin Cover-up: Child Abuse, Satanism and Murder in Nebraska.*[73]

Gunderson played a leading role "in the exposure of the satanic/sexual cover-up in the McMartin Preschool case (Manhattan Beach, California) which had involved over 450 children in the 3–5-year-old range over a period of years." It involved "international child kidnapping, sex slavery, child auctions, satanism & the sale of body parts."[74] After six years of criminal trials, and a change of state senators, no convictions were obtained, and all charges were dropped in 1990.[75]

While the issue of satanic abuse has been highly contested for centuries, we are currently seeing a rise in satanism in Canada. According to Wikipedia,[76] satanism is "a group of ideological and philosophical beliefs based on Satan. Contemporary religious practices of satanism began with the founding of the...Church of Satan...in the United States in 1966."[77] It is becoming a mainline movement opposing the Christian values of the sanctity of life and moral purity. As might be expected, the adherents of this movement, satanists, deny any allegation aimed at them that

---

72   DeCamp, 2011
73   DeCamp, 2011
74   Ibid.
75   DeCamp, 2011
76   "Satanism," Wikipedia, n.d.
77   Ibid.

have to do with satanic rituals and the sexual perversions that accompany them. As more and more former cult members come forward, we're beginning to get a clearer picture and a better understanding of their practices, and equally importantly, their funding. How do we fight back?

Law enforcement agencies worldwide are keenly aware of the child trafficking industry where children in refugee camps are kidnapped and sold as slaves. These slave traders are forever looking for opportunities to harvest children. They are human parasites who prey on the weak and most vulnerable, especially immediately after a catastrophic disaster. This is their time to feast. What can be done about it?

Sex slavery has never in all of history been more widespread than it is today. Unfortunately, given the size and scope of their reach and with their many allies in upper echelons of government and the media, even when tracked down and exposed, these predators are seldom convicted or brought to justice. Jeffrey Epstein is a case in point. Child exploitation is a cancer that keeps growing. When politicians try to do something about it, they are soon met with ferocious and unrelenting opposition. Former U.S. president Donald Trump is a perfect example.

Say what you will about Donald Trump, he tried to help the most vulnerable—children. There is little doubt that one of the primary reasons there was such an effort to get rid of him was because he took measures and issued orders to have abusers of children convicted. Was he getting too close? I suppose we may never know. I have my own thoughts on the matter, and you can probably guess what they might be. Nonetheless, concerted efforts must be made to expose and convict these vile perpetrators.

Over the past few years more has come to light with regards to the sexual abuse of celebrities. One of those is singer Alanis Morissette, now 47, disclosed being sexually abused by several men as a young teenager during her earliest years of fame.

In an article by Steven Zeitchik in the *Washington Post*, Morrisette is quoted saying: "They're all pedophiles. It's all statutory rape."[78]

Although she does not name her alleged abusers she says she tried reaching out for help, but her requests seemed to fall on deaf ears in the music industry. When she did reach out, she claimed people would just stand up and walk out on her."[79]

---

78   Zeitchik, 2021
79   Ibid.

38

Child Abuse, Satanism, Murder, & Injustice on a Grand Scale

During my ex-husband's trial, a story south of our border was unfolding.

In 1990 Alisha Owen testified before a grand jury that she was sexually abused as a juvenile and had also witnessed the abuse of other children.

> The *Chicago Tribune* reported that all nine children tell the same grisly story, of being abused and made to partake in rituals by the school administrator. Police conducted 150 interviews but cannot substantiate the claims! Having once been a skeptic myself, I am in principle no longer willing to dismiss any allegation of child abuse. As more children are encouraged to step forward to expose child predators, police are encountering more cases of child abuse.

> While almost all of the investigation team agreed that these children had been traumatized, the prosecutor, Stanley Levco, didn't agree and proceeded to do his best to publicly clear the accused, the perpetrators.

What about the victims? Unfortunately, this case of child abuse, like so many, was sullied by a system that claims to care, but based on the evidence, doesn't really. A case in point, after almost three years of investigation into the Franklin Case, from 1988 to 1991, it was dropped but never taken up by the newly elected legislature. Why not?[80]

John DeCamp, a lawyer and author of *The Franklin Cover-up,* served for sixteen years as Nebraska state senator, 1971–1987. He stated that for anyone seeking it, there was sufficient evidence available corroborating the victims' testimonies.[81]

He provided Gary Caradori with information, much of which was readily available to anyone willing to research the case. Caradori was, according to WebHarvest/LiveLeak: Redefining the Media (n.d.), an "investigator for the Nebraska State Legislature."[82] Shortly thereafter, Caradori reported that he had received threats, that he had had his phone tapped and his vehicles tampered with. At a barbecue hosted by concerned citizens outraged at the lack of serious investigation into the case, Caradori told the Concerned Parents president that he was selling his boat for fear that it might be tampered with. Unfortunately for him, it wasn't the boat that was tampered with, but his plane.

In July 1990 Caradori, with new evidence in hand, phoned then-Senator [Loran] Schmit, and exclaimed, "We've got them. There's no way they can get out now!"[83] During that same telephone conversation, he informed the senator that he and his son

80   DeCamp, 1996
81   Ibid.
82   https://www.webharvest.gov/congress112th/20130110101607/http://www.liveleak.com/view?i=795_1174761584
83   DeCamp, 1996

were going to fly to Chicago. On July 11, Senator Schmit received a phone call informing him of Gary's death.

Flying back from Chicago, Caradori's plane crashed. A farmer reported seeing a flash of light, hearing an explosion, and seeing the plane plunge to the ground. Both Gary and his son were killed.[84] Was this an accident or a planned murder? You decide, but the evidence, while circumstantial, is compelling.

Caradori had shared with his brother that there were a lot of big names involved and he hoped that even with all their money they wouldn't be able to sweep it all under the rug. The day after his death, FBI agents descended on his home and seized all his records. It remains a mystery as to what was found. However, some names involved had already been leaked.

According Loretta Smith, one of the abuse victims, the names revealed were:

- Larry King (not the TV reporter), manager of the Franklin Credit Union, who apparently had a preference for boys
- a modelling photographer paid by King
- leaders from the North Omaha Girls Club, including prominent doctors and lawyers, who were involved photographing nude children
- a school principal
- foster parents Jarrett and Barbara Webb, and others

In 1988 Loretta provided information linking some of the names in Caradori's list to involvement in cult activities which included the killings of several young children. She gave hospital staff

---

84   Ibid.

detailed information of her involvement with this sick band of creeps.

Loretta was nine when, attending a local girls' club, she was be-friended by "Ray," who, along with other men, would take her and four or five other kids on outings to an abandoned building. There they would encourage the kids to talk about their problems, gaining the children's confidence. This went on for several weeks. It wasn't long before the children were offered joints to get them high. Once "wasted," the girls were forced to "sleep" with the men and were threatened not to tell anyone or they would killed. This went on for about six months.

[85]Abuse wasn't enough, though. As she recounts, the horrors got much worse. She went on to describe being locked in a room with a small infant. Round midnight, men entered the room and killed the baby ritual-style. She was then locked in with the baby's corpse. There are many similar accounts of atrocities that Loretta was witness to, including kidnappings, sex abuse, drug abuse, and the ritualistic murder of children. The director of the Foster Care Review board claimed that these horrifying ac-counts were accurate and corroborated the information already in the hand of the authorities.[86] So what was the end result of the investigation?

The grand jury actually indicted one of the *victims* for perjury. Ali-sha Owen was sentenced to nine to thirteen years. She and another victim, Paul Bonacci, refused to recant.[87]

Dr. Judianne Densen-Gerber, a lawyer, psychiatrist, and nationally prominent specialist on child abuse, retorted, "If the children are

85   Ibid.
86   DeCamp, 1996
87   Ibid.

not telling the truth, particularly if they have been abused, they need help, medical attention. You don't throw them in jail" (De-Camp, 1996, p. xvii).[88]

The system seemed to bend over in protection of the perpetrators against credible victims. Our system of justice seems to be upside down, where evil is now accepted as good and good is deemed evil. The guilty go free to continue harming while the victims are locked up for "talking." Something is dreadfully wrong.

In 1982, *Reader's Digest* reported that an estimated one hundred thousand children are "unaccounted" for each year. The FBI reported on the number of stolen vehicles, homicides, reported rapes, and robberies, but couldn't provide reliable statistics on the number of children disappearing yearly.[89] Fortunately, in 2022 the populace is much more aware of the reality of child abduction and the explosion of the child sex slavery market.

Stardom & Deviance

Another important case came to its conclusion in 2019, when Keith Raniere, founder of NXIVM, was sentenced to 120 years in prison[90] for crimes including racketeering, sex trafficking, forced labor, identity theft, and the sexual exploitation of a child.[91]

NXIVM was a recruiting platform for a "secret society called DOS" in which women were branded and forced into sexual

---

88 Ibid.
89 Ibid.
90 NXIVM leader Keith Raniere sentenced to 120 years in prison | CBC News
91 Nicki Clyne: What Happened to NXIVM Member and Where Is She Now? (newsweek.com)

slavery. In twenty years, over sixteen thousand individuals were ca-joled into taking part.[92]

According to reports, women were kept on starvation diets, brand-ed with Raniere's initials,[93] and ordered to have sex with him. For-mer members testified that they were punished with long-term confinement and whippings.

Prior to Raniere's conviction, five actresses of his inner circle who had been charged with a long list of crimes had pled guilty.[94] These included: Allison Mack (*Smallville*);[95] Nicki Clyne (*Battlestar Galactica*);[96] Canadian Sarah Edmondson (*Stargate SG-1*);[97] Grace Park (*A Million Little Things*);[98] and India Oxenberg, daughter of Catherine Oxenberg (*Dynasty*).[99] According to the Cinema-holic website, Edmondson chose to join NXIVM and went on to become one of their top recruiters, "recruiting more than 2,000 members."[100]

---

92 Here Are All the Major Players in the NXIVM Case | Time; "Keith Raniere," Wikipedia, n.d.

93 "Keith Raniere," Wikipedia, n.d.

94 Here Are All the Major Players in the NXIVM Case | Time

95 Smallville actress Allison Mack pleads guilty to charges related to alleged sex cult NXIVM | CBC News

96 Nicki Clyne: What Happened to NXIVM Member and Where Is She Now? (newsweek.com)

97 Vancouver woman who escaped NXIVM sex cult relieved with lead-er's 120-year prison sentence | CBC News; https://www.imdb.com/title/tt0118480/characters/nm0249550

98 NXIVM: Allison Mack, Grace Park and Other Actors Recruited by the Cult | Entertainment Tonight (etonline.com)

99 Ibid.

100 https://thecinemaholic.com/where-is-sarah-edmondson-now/

Over twelve victims gave testimonies at the trial of manipulation and abuse. As is typical of many predators, Raniere was a master manipulator who preyed on the vulnerable in plain sight.

part five

PROTECT YOUR CHILDREN

39

Secure Attachment

Today, the world is a far different place than it was in the 60s. Psychologically, we have a far deeper understanding of the psyche of young children, particularly their need for a sense of security, the need of "attachment."

In 1958, attachment theory was a fledging study. Even though change came slowly, John Bowlby's[101] and Mary Ainsworth's[102] research helped to influence how children and their parents were treated in hospital.

John Bowlby, a British psychologist, psychiatrist, and psychoanalyst, is recognized for his work on child development and his pioneering work on attachment theory. Child wartime trauma and the separation of children from parents and/or caregivers during WWII had a significant influence on his work. He studied the effects of separation on Jewish children rescued from the horrors of the concentration camps as well as children who had been evacuated from London so that women could help in the war effort.[103]

Bowlby's interest in the study of "separation" was influenced by

---

101   Bowlby, 1969
102   Ainsworth et al., 1978
103   Bowlby, 1944, 1969

Anna Freud and Dorothy Burlingham's work with evacuees as well as Rene Spitz's work with orphans. By the late 1950s, Bowlby had accumulated a body of empirical evidence demonstrating the importance of physical human attachment from birth.[104] What interactive patterns were needed for healthy physical and mental development of the individual? What he discovered was that attachment behaviour is, right from birth, a survival strategy, and the need for it is a characteristic in all humans.

In collaboration, Bowlby and his student, Mary Ainsworth, took his ideas a step farther in order to demonstrate the validity of his findings. Ainsworth suggested that several attachment styles existed.[105] Together, their research demonstrated clearly what happens when young children are uprooted from their parents.[106]

According to Ainsworth, attachment behaviour is any form of behaviour that results in a person attempting or retaining proximity to some other differentiated and preferred individual, who is usually perceived as stronger and/or wiser. Although it is most frequently and most intensely displayed by infants and young children, it continues to be manifested throughout life, especially when one is distressed, ill, or frightened.[107]

The charts below compare and contrast what might be referred to as a safe environment eliciting positive attachment behaviour, as in Figure 1, with Figure 2, which is considered a less safe environment that will most likely elicit negative attachment behaviour. Ideally, parents, caregivers, and social agencies should implement measures and offer environments that emulate the cycle as shown in Figure 1. Unfortunately, many children are traumatized by exposure to

---

104   Bowlby, 1977; Ainsworth, 1984, p. 792
105   Karen, 1998
106   Grossman et al., 2005
107   Ainsworth, 1984, in R. Karen, 1994

the cycle as shown in Figure 2. Their trauma may be a result of losing a parent, having been taken out of the home, or having been abused.

The following charts (Figures 1 and 2), adapted from Bunce and Rickards (2004),[108] help to synthesize the statement above.

Sroufe (2010) makes it clear that accumulated risk factors in early childhood are a significant predictor of behavioural problems in middle childhood or early adolescence, even if the risks in middle childhood and beyond are mitigated.[109]

---

108   Bunce, M., & Rickards, A. (2004). *Working with bereaved children: A guide.* Rachel Harvey (Ed.). Retrieved from http://www.essex.ac.uk/ARMEDCON/unit/projects/wwbc_guide/
109   Sroufe, 2010

THE AROUSAL-RELAXATION CYCLE

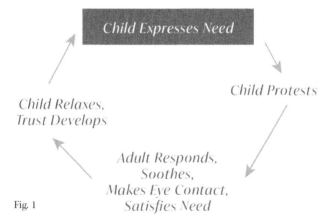

Fig. 1

THE DISTURBED ATTACHMENT CYCLE

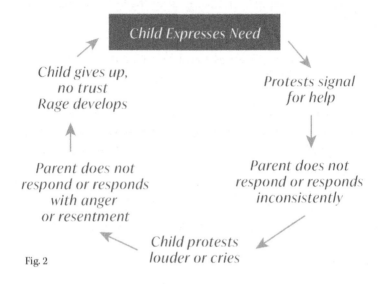

Fig. 2

In other words, what a child experiences in early childhood may well influence their behaviour later in life. Therefore, the impact of childhood experiences on their adult life cannot be overstated. My life and the lives of my children bear this out.

The greatest protection your child can experience is that of a secure, loving home with a mentally healthy mother and father. While this is the ideal, it is not always possible. Creating the very best loving home, with good boundaries and healthy respect for all, will go a long way in protecting your child from predators.

Nevertheless, vigilance on the part of parents and caregivers can pay huge dividends in the life of the child. Don't be afraid to monitor and challenge their access to social media and friends and what they are learning in the classrooms. The children under your care are precious gifts that you have been given and that you are responsible for.

part six

RESTORING THE MOSAIC

40

Beauty from Ashes

Leaving the topic of pedophilia in the marketplace, I want to share our family's personal journey of healing and restoration.

Two years into my second marriage, I told my husband of my desire to go back to school to learn how I might help our children. He agreed. Little did we know the years of education before us.

My Journey into Healing on the Nine-week Course

In the second semester of my bachelor degree, I was fortunate to be able to attend a Christian program focused on emotional healing. From the moment I walked in the doors, I knew it was going to be challenging.

The third night there, I dreamt of the Angel of the Lord standing over a heavy cement well lid. It looked just like the cement lid over our old well when I was a child. The angel was beginning to lift it and I remember yelling, *"No! No!"* There was no way I wanted to see what was under that lid. I argued with the angel, but in my spirit I knew that I wanted to say yes. He obviously did too as the lid opened

I could see a small bedraggled girl of about six in a muddy dress at the bottom of the well. I knew her. She was *me*. I wanted the lid shut immediately, but God wanted it open, and so this was a short-lived conflict. God in His wisdom was beginning to cleanse the vile stain on my heart.

I knew that this was going to be a difficult and emotionally costly road to follow, but in those nine weeks I was exposed to some of the best Christian teaching I had ever heard. As I experienced the deep love of God, I found I was able to forgive my father, my mother, my ex-husband, and many others. I thought I had forgiven them before, but this was a deeper cleansing than I had ever experienced. The wounded child within began a process of deep healing and restoration.

For me, this time of teaching and restoration set the backdrop for my counselling career. Although my professional training is in psychology, the profound experiences and training I had during this program allowed me to help others in a deeply profound way in their own journeys of healing.

My undergrad studies focused on two areas: childhood sexual abuse and same-sex attraction. I continued this focus for my master's and Ph.D., with the addition of a third element to my studies: attachment theory. I completed two internships in Emotionally Focused Therapy and Adult Attachment Inventory—a qualitative research assessment tool.

Prior to my university studies, I hadn't even completed high school. I was in grade 11 when I left home at seventeen. Returning to school at the university level at age thirty-eight stretched me considerably. I was a mother of six, two of whom were very young. When I started university I never in my wildest dreams thought I would continue beyond my undergrad studies. But something stirred inside me and kept pushing me. I continued my education, completing my masters of professional counselling, and continued in private practice, returning to complete my Ph.D. in 2014.

It seemed that whenever I was attending university one of the children would be in crisis. Not long after I attended the nine-week course, Daniel, who was nineteen at the time and living in London, Ontario, was in a downhill spiral with drugs. We were camping when we received a phone call from the charge nurse at the London hospital.

Daniel had arrived with no vital signs present after a drug overdose, and although they had resuscitated him, they told us that they were not expecting him to live. As we drove the two hours to the London hospital, I prayed for God's hand of healing but at the same time planned my son's funeral.

When we arrived, his brother and sister were standing by his bedside and Daniel was sitting up in bed as though nothing had happened. I wanted to hug him and hit him in the same moment. One would have hoped that given the pain and suffering he had caused to himself and our family, he would come to his senses and stop his destructive ways. Unfortunately, this experience did nothing to curtail his or his elder brother's drug habits. If anything, the two of them delved more deeply into the drug scene. The hopes and dreams I had for my handsome, creative, intelligent, and gifted sons were dashed.

Garnet became immersed in a lifestyle of drugs and sexual promiscuity, while Daniel involved himself in drugs, theft, and lawlessness. Our visit to the London hospital wouldn't be the last time our hearts felt shattered as our children tried to find ways to cope with their inner pain.

All three of my children have fought a self-destructive battle since their childhood. While Ava and Garnet have, for the most part, moved past the horrible residues of the past thanks to trauma counselling, Daniel still has moments that lead him to the brink. I am continually thankful to God his life has been repeatedly spared.

Ava was my dream child, and although we butted heads many times during her teen years, she grew into a beautiful, kind, and successful woman, graduating from nursing college and marrying her high school sweetheart. As I write this, in fact, it is their twentieth wedding anniversary. Staying married to the same person for twenty years is quite an accomplishment in this day and age.

The emotional pain of knowing your children are suffering has definitely taken its toll. The years seem to have flown by as time always does when one looks in the mirror of one's life. Through it all, Bob has remained a rock, speaking truth and hope into my life when I felt like the proverbial sky was falling. My deepest comfort in my darkest hours, though, belongs to God, who has given me hope where there was no hope.

My Children - Lingering Effects of Trauma & Poor Decisions

Garnet left behind a life that had been stealing his soul and his peace and severing his relationship with God. He made some very difficult decisions and began his journey back from the brink. He is now married with four beautiful children.

In the meantime, Daniel's first marriage was coming to an end during my Ph.D. years. We had hoped that he and his wife could work through issues, but he had continued choosing drugs over family and she was finished. He was devastated by the loss of his family and once again spiraled into the drug pit. Daniel's addictions once more took control. He was arrested on drug charges and spent six months in a provincial jail, where he was violently beaten by eight guards. That was only the beginning. As a result of the beating, Daniel now suffers from epileptic seizures and migraine headaches. He was out of jail for only a little while, and then came the news that he had been arrested again, this time for driving without a license, theft, mischief, and multiple other charges. He was sent this time to Millhaven in Kingston, Ontario—a maximum security penitentiary.

What few emotional resources I had left were on the verge of collapse. I was angry with him, with God, and with myself. I had a crisis of faith. I had prayed for each of my children since the time they were in my womb. I had prayed for them each night of their lives. Yet this was what God allowed? He had not protected my older three from their own father! My anger toward God grew as the circumstances worsened, and with it a level of despair I had never encountered before.

Daniel was transferred to another prison, where he was attacked by an inmate with a switchblade. It felt like I was losing all hope. Would he be returned to us alive? The outcome of the assault, though, was an answer to prayer. When prison officials reviewed the tape of the incident and interviewed witnesses, they found that he had been a constant target while in prison. The decision was made to transfer him to a medium-security facility.

While I was preparing for my dissertation, and in the summer before he started university, Luke, our youngest, was arrested for being drunk and disorderly after a party. While the charge in and of itself was minor, because he twice breached the conditions of his probation to jail he went. For me, it was another stomach blow. What had I done so wrong? This boy had not suffered at the hands of a pedophilic father. He'd had a secure, loving home with a great dad and so many advantages that my older children never had. I was exhausted and beyond devastated. I was plagued with guilt and shame, especially as I had placed so much hope in this son. And he was heading down the drug and party scene of his brothers, which he had watched from afar.

All the years of uncertainty, pain, and distress for my children came to a climax. In my third year of university, I suffered from burnout. I had to cut back my client load to half and reduce my enrolment to part time. It took almost three years for me to recover and five years of study and research to complete my postgraduate studies, finally earning my Ph.D.

Ongoing Ministry

Thanks to the grace of God my children are being restored. It is for them, like us all, a work in progress. I have been able to pursue the purpose that God has called me to. The storms help to shape us into the leaders God intends us to be, if we will not give up or grow weary. We are not only to survive but to thrive in the midst of the storm.

Although I had intended to avoid the topic of same-sex attraction during my Ph.D. studies, it was not to be. I had planned my dissertation to be on child sexual abuse (CSA). After all, CSA was an academically accepted focus, whereas a dissertation on homosexuality was likely to draw intense scrutiny and censorship from academia and outright hatred from the LGBTQ community. Nevertheless, it felt like God had put a fire in my heart for this community and for those who sought to change their behaviour.

My dissertation was titled *An Exploration of Early Childhood Attachment in a Sample of Christian Men Experiencing Same-Sex Attraction.*[110, 111]

In 2016 I wrote *Deep Impact: Integrating Theology and Psychology in the Treatment of Complex Traumatic Stress,*[112] followed the next year by *Closing the Floodgates: Setting the Record Straight on Gender and Sexuality.*[113]

I continued to work in private practice until 2019, at which time I retired from counselling to pursue writing and a speaking career as well as advocating on behalf of the vulnerable.

You can find me online at restoringthemosiac.ca

110   Gillies, 2016
111   Restoring the Mosaic | Education, Advocacy and Social Action for True Gender And Sexuality
112   Gillies, 2016
113   Gillies, 2017

A CALL TO ACTION

41

A Call to Action

As you can imagine, this has not been an easy book to write. Tears have flowed as the words spilled out. Hugs for my children have been readily dispensed. Hugs don't make the memories go away, but they do help in healing.

If at any time you have felt that I am being hard on a particular group of people, it's only because it is my desire to expose evil. I have read too much research and heard too many personal testimonies to ignore the reality that there is definite linkage between radicals within the LGBTQ community and the promotion of pedophilia.

The truth needs to be exposed. I cannot remain silent when truth is denied. The promotion of pedophilia within academia, social media, and even mainstream media is nothing short of criminal. Journalists have become narrative defenders rather than purveyors of truth.

The invasive, confusing, and morally repugnant indoctrination of our children within the public education system is sinister and unprecedented. In 2017, I was still holding out hope that parents would awaken in time to change the school system. I no longer hold to that hope—at least in Canada. We are so far down an educational "rabbit hole" that I fear there is no return for the public

241

school system as it now stands. Catholic schools fare no better, and many private schools are following suit. The infusion of pornographic materials and the promotion of ideologically driven sex education based on false premises is creating a mental health crisis in our youth.

Our children and grandchildren are being radically groomed by those meant to protect them. They are being desensitized by inappropriate sexualized content from multiple sources, opening them up to increased levels of suggestibility and vulnerability. The outcome of such evil will become manifest in their lives as they mature into adulthood.

Where sexual boundaries are removed, a free-for-all ensues. Any and all forms of sexual expression are deemed acceptable, paving the way for pedophilia to become an epidemic in our lifetime. In fact, I believe we are already experiencing this, as seen in almost daily news accounts of sex rings, sex slavery, and pedophilic exposure.

I currently work with a small group of informed individuals to bring presentations to pastors and political leaders. I plan to continue with my research and to speak out in the "marketplace" about the atrocities happening to our children, including the medicalizing of children in the transgender revolution.

So what are the next steps? Action!

In order to see change, parents and grandparents need to get involved. We must rescue our children before it's too late. Maybe you think I'm exaggerating. If so, please check the books and assignments your children are given both in the classroom and in the library. Sit in their classes.

Along with accessing curricula, please read extensively on the subject and talk with teachers. I encourage you to run for public office municipally, provincially, or federally. You are probably thinking, *I could never do that*. I felt the same way, until I felt the tug to run for office in our riding. Did I win? No! I was disallowed because of my stance on subjects as revealed in my books. But intending to run for federal office started me on a journey of activism.

Informed and concerned parents from all walks of life are desperately needed in a multitude of positions across our communities. Remember, when good people don't get involved, evil ones will. Consider running for school board or a local parents' advisory board. This is a critically important role. You can help mould the minds of children and grandchildren.

Get involved. It's time to *unite* and restore morality in our culture. Parents need to rise up and take back what has been usurped from them: their God-given role to raise their children as first and primary educators. We must turn back the tide or soon the tsunami will overwhelm us.

ABOUT THE AUTHOR

ANN E. GILLIES, PH.D., is a retired marriage and family therapist, trauma specialist, pastor, international speaker, and advocate for protecting our most vulnerable. Her private practice of twenty-five years was made up primarily of clients seeking treatment for childhood sexual abuse and symptoms of complex traumatic stress disorder.

Ann's presentations and workshops include: Complex Traumatic Stress Disorder, Conflict Resolution, Emotional Regulation, Detection and Prevention of Childhood Sexual Abuse, Gender and Sexuality, The Transgender Phenomenon, Psychological First Aid, and Post-Traumatic Stress Disorder. She has hosted many marriage and family retreats and taught several counselling, marriage, and family courses.

Ann and her husband, Bob, have a blended family of six adult children, three of whom were subjected to child sexual abuse at the hands of her former husband and, as a result, suffer the long-term consequences of complex trauma.

Bob and Ann are now proud grandparents to twelve wonderful grandchildren and one great-grandchild.

This book is a tribute to all those who struggle with the rippling and often tsunami-like effects of the traumatic experiences of their lives. They are the survivors.

You can find her website at restoringthemosaic.ca

REFERENCES

Abel, G.G., and Harlow, N. (2009). "What 44,000 adult males and 12,000 boys with troubled sexual histories show us about preventing child sexual abuse." Paper presented at the California Coalition on Sexual Offending / National Conference on Child Sexual Abuse and Exploitation Prevention, San Francisco, May 16, 2009.

Ainsworth, M.D.S., Blehar, M.C., Waters, E., & Wall, S. (1978). *Patterns of attachment: A psychological study of the strange situation.* Hillsdale, N.J.: Erlbaum Publications.

Ainsworth, M.D.S. (1984). "Attachments across the life span." Bulletin of the New York Academy of Medicine, 61, 792–812. In R. Karen (1994), *Becoming attached: First relationships and how they shape our capacity to love.* New York: Oxford University Press.

American Psychiatric Association. (2013). *Diagnostic and statistical manual of mental disorders* (5th ed.). Washington, DC: Author.

American Psychological Association. (2013). APA statement regarding pedophilia and the DSM-5

Andriette, B. (1999). The Guide. http://archive.guidemag.com/index.cfm

B4U-ACT. (n.d.) www.b4uact.org/know-the-facts.

Barrier, D. (n.d.) Male Sex Offenders (child-abuse-effects.com)

Benson, G.T. (2021). Well-known veterinarian charged with child porn and 'animal crushing' had sex with dogs, feds say—Breaking911

Bindel, J. (2015, September). "Britain's Apologists for Child Abuse."

Bowlby, J. (1944). Forty-four juvenile thieves: Their characters and home lives. *International Journal of Psychoanalysis,* Vol. 25, p. 19–52.

247

Bowlby, J. (1969). *Attachment and loss.* Vol. 1. Hogarth Press and the Institute of Psychoanalysis. In Bowlby, J. (1997). *Attachment and Loss.* Australia: Random House, p. 233.

Bowlby, J. (1977). *Maternal Care and Mental Health.* Jason Aronson Inc. Publishers.

Bunce, M., and Rickards, A. (2004). "Working with Bereaved Children: A Guide." Department for International Development: the Children's Legal Centre, www.essex.ac.uk/armedcon/unit/projects/wwbc_guide/index.html

Burke, M. (2021). https://www.msn.com/en-us/news/us/essentially-child-pornography-ohio-mayor-asks-school-board-to-resign-over-racy-assignments/ar-AAOtHSF

Cacciatori, H. (2017). "The Lived Experiences of Men Attracted to Minors and Their Therapy-Seeking Behaviors." https://scholarworks.waldenu.edu/cgi/viewcontent.cgi?article=4970&context=dissertations

"Camille Paglia." (n.d.) Wikipedia.

Cash, B.M. (2016). "Self-Identifications, Sexual Development, and Wellbeing in Minor-Attracted People: An Exploratory Study" (master's thesis). Cornell University, Ithaca, NY.

DeCamp, J. (2011). *The Franklin Cover-up: Child Abuse, Satanism, and Murder in Nebraska,* second edition, pp. xvii–23. Lincoln, NE: A W T, Incorporated.

Diamond, L., and Rosky, C.J. (2016). "Scrutinizing Immutability: Research on Sexual Orientation and U.S. Legal Advocacy for Sexual Minorities." https://pubmed.ncbi.nlm.nih.gov/26986464/

Edwards, A. (2017). Yes Mom, There is Something Wrong | by Anthony Edwards | Medium

Edwards, J. (2019). "Arrest and Prosecution of Animal Sex Abuse (Bestiality) Offenders in the United States, 1975–2015." *Journal of the American Academy of Psychiatry and the Law,* 47(3). JAAPL.003836-19; DOI: https://doi.org/10.29158/JAAPL.003836-19

English, K., Jones, L., Patrick, D., and Pasini-Hill, D. (2003). "Sexual offender containment: use of the post-conviction polygraph." *Annals of New York Academy of Sciences* 989, 411–27.

Fink, P.J., Silberg, J., and Whitfield, C.L., eds. (2001). *Misinformation Concerning Child Sexual Abuse and Adult Survivors*. Haworth Maltreatment & Trauma Press. p. 129. ISBN 9780789019004

Finkelhor, D. (1993). "Epidemiological factors in the clinical identification of child sexual abuse." *Child Abuse & Neglect*, 17, 67–70.

Freimond, C.M. (2009). "Navigating the Stigma of Pedophilia: The Experiences of Nine Minor-Attracted Men in Canada" (master's thesis). Simon Fraser University, British Columbia, Canada.

Gamson, J. (1997). "Messages of Exclusion: Gender, Movements, and Symbolic Boundaries." *Gender and Society*, 11(2), 178–199.

Gebhard, P.H., Gagnon, J.H., Pomeroy, W.B., and Christenson, C.V. (1965). *Sex Offenders: An Analysis of Types*. New York: Harper & Row and Paul B. Hoeber, Inc., Medical Books.

Gillies, A.E. (2016). An Exploration of a Sample of Christian Men Experiencing Same-Sex Attraction (researchgate.net).

Gillies, A.E. (2017). *Closing the Floodgates: Setting the Record Straight on Gender and Sexuality*. Winnipeg, Manitoba, Canada: Word Alive Publishing.

Goode, S. (2010). *Understanding and Addressing Adult Sexual Attraction to Children: A study of paedophiles in contemporary society*, pp. 6–8. Oxford, UK: Routledge.

Grossman, K.E., Grossman, K., and Waters, E. (2005). *Attachment from Infancy to Adulthood*. New York: Guildford Press.

Hopper, J. (n.d.) Jim Hopper, PH.D. | Facts About Sexual Abuse of Boys

International Pedophile and Child Emancipation. (n.d.) ipce.info

"John Bowlby." (n.d.) Wikipedia.

Kantor, K. (2015). People You May Know. https://www.youtube.com/
watch?v=LoyfunmYIpU

Kaplan, M. (2014). "Pedophilia: A Disorder, Not a Crime." https://www.
nytimes.com/2014/10/06/opinion/pedophilia-a-disorder-not-a-
crime.html

Karen, R. (1998). *Becoming Attached: First Relationships and How They Shape
Our Capacity to Love.* Oxford, UK: Oxford University Press.

"Keith Raniere." (n.d.) Wikipedia.

Kessler, R.C., McLaughlin, K.A., Green, J.G., Gruber, M.J., Sampson, N.A.,
Zaslavsky, A.M., et al. (2010). "Childhood adversities and adult
psychopathology in the WHO world mental health surveys." *British
Journal of Psychiatry*, 197(5), 3783–85.

Kinsey, A.C., Pomeroy, W.P., and Martin, C. E. (1948). *Sexual Behavior in the
Human Male.* Bloomington, IN: Indiana University Press.

Levitt, L., Hoffer, T.A., and Loper, A.B. (2016). "Criminal histories of a sub-
sample of animal cruelty offenders." *Aggression and Violent Behavior*,
30, 48–58.

MacFarlane, K., and Waterman, J. (1986). *Sexual Abuse of Young Children:
Evaluation and Treatment*, p. 9. New York: The Guilford Press.

"North American Man/Boy Love Association." (n.d.) Conservapedia.

"North American Man/Boy Love Association." (n.d.) Wikipedia.

"NXIVM." (n.d.) Wikipedia.

O'Carroll, T. (1980). *Paedophilia: The radical case.* London, UK: Owen Publishing.

Paglia, C. (1991). *Sexual Personae*, illustrated edition, p. 116. New York:
Vintage.

Paglia, C. (2014). "The Drinking Age Is Past Its Prime." *The Telegraph*. Archived March 6, 2014.

Pedersen, M.R. (2017). "The Politics of being a Pedophile." https://www.b4uact.org/wp-content/uploads/2014/12/The-Politics-of-being-a-Pedophile.pdf

Perry, B.D. (2003). "Effects of traumatic events on children." The Child Trauma Academy. Retrieved from www.childtrauma.org

Phillips, M. (1993). Operation Monarch. Operation Monarch (outpost-of-freedom.com)

Plummer, K. (1991). "Understanding childhood sexualities." *Journal of Homosexuality*, 20(1-2), 231–249.

Pomeroy, W.B. (1976, November). "A new look at incest." Penthouse Forum, 9–13; Variations Magazine (1977) 86–88; Forum Magazine (1976, November), 84–89.

Porter, D. Pedophilic Disorder DSM-5 302.2 (F65.4). https://www.theravive.com/therapedia/pedophilic-disorder-dsm--5-302.2-(f65.4)

Reisman, J., et al. (1990). *Kinsey, Sex, and Fraud: The Indoctrination of a People*. Lafayette, LA: Lochinvar-Huntington House.

Reisman, J. (2003). *Stolen Honor, Stolen Innocence*. Orlando, FL: New Revolution Publishers.

"Satanism." (n.d.) Wikipedia.

Seto, M.C. (2017) "The puzzle of male chronophilias." Arch Sex Behaviour, 46(1), 3–22.

Siegel, E.L. (2021). Boy Scouts reach $850 million settlement with tens of thousands of sexual abuse victims (nbcnews.com)

Simons, D.A., Wurtele, S.K., Durham, R.L. (2008). "Developmental experiences of child sexual abusers and rapists." *Child Abuse & Neglect*, 32, 549–60.

Soto, O.R. (2005). "FBI targets pedophilia advocates: Little-known group promotes 'benevolent' sex" *San Diego Union-Tribune*, 18 February.

Sroufe, L.A., Coffino, B., Carlson, E.A. (2010). "Conceptualizing the role of early experience: Lessons from the Minnesota longitudinal study." *Developmental Review*, 30(1), 36–51.

Swift, M. "The Gay Revolutionary." (1987). First printed in *Gay Community News*, February 15–21 (1987); reprinted from The Congressional Record of the United States Congress (2016).

Trueman, C. (2020). *The Rise and Triumph of the Modern Self*, p. 204. Wheaton, IL: Crossway Books.

Vachss, A. (1998). Testimony of Andrew Vachss before the United States National Commission on Libraries and Information Science. http://www.vachss.com/av_dispatches/testimony.html

Vachss, A. (2013). "Confusing Ideation with Criminal Action: The difference between a pedophile and a predatory pedophile is a criminal act." http://www.vachss.com/av_dispatches/predatory.html

Vogt, H. (2006). The Leipziger Study of the Social and Psychical Situation of Pedophilic Men. Pabst Science Publishers, Lengerich. https://www.ipce.info/host/vogt/vogt_content.htm

Zeitchik, S. (2021). Alanis Morissette makes allegations of statutory rape in new HBO movie—The Washington Post

Made in the USA
Middletown, DE
10 February 2023

23688997R00150